The
Life of Prophet
Muhammad [PBUH]

By:

Hadhrat Moulana Siddeeq Ahmad Baandwi Saheb رحمة الله عليه

Title: The Life of Prophet Muhammad [PBUH] ﷺ

By: Hadhrat Moulana Siddeeq Ahmad Baandwi Saheb رحمة الله عليه

Prepared by:
Jamiatul Ulama (KZN)
Ta'limi Board
4 Third Avenue

P.O.Box 26024
Isipingo Beach
4115
South Africa

First edition:	Rajab	1426 /	July	2005
Second edition:	Muharram	1427 /	February	2006
Third edition:	Shaban	1428 /	August	2007

Published By : The Way of Islam, 6 Cave Street, Preston, Lancashire, PR1 4SP

Contents

Preface

In every era numerous authors have written books of various sizes on the seerah (life) of Nabi ﷺ. This service is still continuing and an assortment of gems will continue to be discovered from this vast ocean.

There is no doubt that this insignificant individual does not possess the expertise required for this field. However, time and again this idea had surfaced that something should be written on this sacred topic regardless of the result with the hope that it may be a means of my salvation in the hereafter.

Thus, I undertook the task of compiling this small book by extracting different aspects from the various books authored on seerah.

I have taken special care to ensure that the language is of an understandable and simple level.

May Allah ﷻ crown this effort with His acceptance and allow it to be beneficial for one and all. May it also be a means of my salvation in the hereafter.

(Hadhrat Qari) Ahqar Siddeeq Ahmad رحمة الله عليه
Khaadim (servant) of Jaami'ah 'Arabiyyah, Hathora, India

13 Shawwaal 1416 A.H.

Birth of Nabi ﷺ

Our Nabi ﷺ was born on Monday, 9th Rabi-ul-Awwal (20th April 571), at the time of subah sadiq (early dawn). Some historians say that his date of birth could have been the 8th or the 12th Rabi-ul-Awwal.

Lineage (Family tree)

Rasulullah's ﷺ father's name was Abdullah. His lineage from his father is as follows:

Muhammad ﷺ bin (the son of) Abdullah bin Abdul Muttalib bin Haashim bin Abd-e-Manaaf bin Qusayy bin Kilaab bin Murrah bin Ka`b bin Lu-ayy bin Ghaalib bin Fahr bin Nadhr bin Kinaanah bin Khuzaimah bin Mudrikah bin Ilyas bin Mudar bin Nizaar bin Ma`add bin A`dnan.

Our Nabi's ﷺ respected mother's name was Aaminah. His lineage from his mother is as follows:

Muhammad ﷺ bin Aaminah bint (daughter of) Wahb bin A`bd-e-Manaf bin Zuhrah bin Kilaab.

Both the families meet at Kilaab and thereafter the lineage is the same.

Nabi's ﷺ paternal grandmother's name was Faatima and his maternal grandmother's name was Barrah. Nabi's ﷺ family and tribe were named the Banu Haashim and Quraish respectively. Nabi ﷺ did not have any brothers or sisters.

Upbringing of Nabi ﷺ

Nabi ﷺ was first breastfed by his mother and then by Thuwaibah, the freed slave of his uncle, Abu Lahab. On receiving the news of his nephew's birth from Thuwaibah, he freed her out of joy.

Thereafter, Nabi ﷺ was breastfed by Haleemah Sa'diyah رضي الله عنها. After two years, Haleemah رضي الله عنها returned Nabi ﷺ to his mother in Makkah but insisted that she wanted to take him back to her home.

Nabi ﷺ would accompany Haleemah's رضي الله عنها sons when they took the goats out to graze. It was during one of these outings that the famous incident of the splitting of Nabi's ﷺ chest by the angel Jibraeel الَّيِّلا occurred. Due to this unusual incident, Haleemah رضي الله عنها became very worried and brought Nabi ﷺ back to Makkah.

Nabi's ﷺ mother passed away when he was only six years old. His grandfather, Abdul Muttalib, then took care of him. After two years, his grandfather also passed away. Thereafter, his uncle Abu Taalib undertook the responsibility of caring for him. Although he lovingly carried out this task till his death, he unfortunately did not accept Islaam.

First journey to Shaam (Syria)

Abu Taalib took Nabi ﷺ with him on a business trip to Syria. On the way they passed a place called Busrah where a Christian monk, by the name of Buhaira, lived. Buhaira approached Nabi ﷺ, looked at him and told Abu Taalib that Nabi ﷺ is indeed the final prophet and that all the signs mentioned in the previous kitaabs (scriptures) are present in him. He also advised that Nabi ﷺ should not be taken to Syria, as the Jews living there may kill him. Abu Taalib accepted his advice and sent Nabi ﷺ back to Makkah.

Second journey to Shaam (Syria)

Hadhrat Khadijah رضي الله عنها was a wealthy lady from the Quraish tribe. She was a widow and traded in different places. She required a trustworthy and intelligent person to run her business. At around this time, Khadija رضي الله عنها had heard the people of Makkah refer to Muhammad ﷺ in excellent and praiseworthy terms. Accordingly she decided to hire Nabi ﷺ as this trustworthy and honourable person was ideally suited to run her business affairs. The first trip that Rasulullah ﷺ undertook for Hadhrat Khadija رضي الله عنها was to Syria where he was put in charge of a trading caravan. She sent her slave Maysarah to assist him.

During this journey, another Christian monk by the name of Nastoorah met Nabi ﷺ under a tree and bore testimony to his nubuwat (prophethood). According to him, only Ambiyaa had previously rested beneath that tree.

Maysarah who accompanied Nabi ﷺ on this journey narrated that whenever it was hot and the rays of the sun struck them, two angels would spread their wings and provide shade to Nabi ﷺ.

Nabi ﷺ sold the goods in quick time with a profit and returned from Syria with more goods. These goods were also sold with a good profit.

First nikah (marriage)

After hearing about the remarkable qualities of our Nabi ﷺ, Hadhrat Khadijah رضي الله عنها sent a proposal for marriage. Nabi's ﷺ paternal uncle accepted it in exchange of a mahr (dowry) of twenty camels. Nabi ﷺ then married Hadhrat Khadijah رضي الله عنها. Some say that the mahr was twelve awqiyas of silver (one awqiya is equal to forty dirhams). Nabi ﷺ was twenty-five years old at that time and Hadhrat Khadijah رضي الله عنها was forty.

Hadhrat Khadijah's رضي الله عنها marriage to Nabi ﷺ lasted for twenty-five years and two and three-quarter months. Nabi ﷺ did not marry any other woman during her lifetime. From Hadhrat Khadijah رضي الله عنها, Nabi ﷺ had four daughters and two sons. The names of the daughters were Zaynab, Umm-e-Kulthoom, Ruqayya and Faatima رضي الله عنهن. The sons names were Qaasim and Taahir رضي الله عنهما. Taahir رضي الله عنه was also referred to as Abdullah.

Nabi ﷺ also had another son by the name of Ibraheem رضي الله عنه who passed away during infancy. He was born from Maariya Qibtiyya رضي الله عنها, the slave woman of Nabi ﷺ. She was given to Nabi ﷺ as a gift by Maqoqas (The ruler of Alexandria).

The names of Nabi's ﷺ honourable wives

1. Hadhrat Khadijah رضي الله عنها
2. Hadhrat Aa'ishah رضي الله عنها
3. Hadhrat Hafsah رضي الله عنها
4. Hadhrat Safiyyah رضي الله عنها
5. Hadhrat Sowda رضي الله عنها
6. Hadhrat Zaynab binte Jahsh رضي الله عنها
7. Hadhrat Zaynub binte Khuzaymah رضي الله عنها
8. Hadhrat Umme Habeebah رضي الله عنها
9. Hadhrat Umme Salimah رضي الله عنها
10. Hadhrat Juwayriyyah رضي الله عنها
11. Hadhrat Maymoonah رضي الله عنها

Character and dealings before nubuwat

There was much evil prevalent in the Arabs before Islaam. Allah ﷻ
protected Nabi ﷺ from every evil. That is why Nabi ﷺ is attributed
with the distinctive quality of the Ambiyaa of being *ma'soom* (sinless).
Nabi's ﷺ akhlaaq (character) was pure and his dealings were
impeccable. Nobody possessed qualities like that of Rasulullah ﷺ. All
the people of Makkah trusted him. They called him **As-Saadiq** (the
truthfull) and **Al-Ameen** (the trustworthy). After Nabi ﷺ received
nubuwat, the mushrikeen would still entrust their *"amaanah"* (trusts)
by him even though they opposed his mission.

Once, a peculiar incident occurred from which we learn how much the
people trusted Nabi ﷺ. The Ka`bah was damaged by a flood and all
the tribes gathered to rebuild the Ka`bah. When the time came to
secure the Hajr-e-Aswad in place, every tribe wished to have this
honour and no solution to this problem could be found. The situation
was tense and it seemed that a war could ensue.

Some people of understanding amongst the Quraish wished to remedy
the situation and prevent this fight. They held a meeting and decided
that the first person to enter the Musjid ul Haraam from a certain door
the following day would make the final decision. Everyone would then
have to accept his decision.

The next day, coincidentally, the first person to enter was Nabi ﷺ.
When the people saw him they were extremely happy and all said
together: "This is As-Saadiq, this is Al-Ameen. He is the best person
among the Arabs and he will make the best decision."

When they presented this dilemma to Nabi ﷺ, he placed the Hajr-e-
Aswad on a piece of cloth and said that certain people from every tribe
should be chosen to carry the cloth to where the black stone was to be
placed.

When they reached the place where the Hajr-e-Aswad was to be placed, Nabi ﷺ picked it up and placed it into position with his own mubaarak hands. Through this excellent decision of Nabi ﷺ, everyone was appeased and no dispute took place.

Risaalat and Nubuwat (Prophethood)

Risaalat means to be a messenger and nubuwat means to be a prophet. Rasools and Nabis are the truthful servants of Allah ﷻ. Allah ﷻ chose them to convey His commands to His servants. They did not make changes to His commands nor did they hide any laws.

The difference between a Nabi and a Rasool

Rasools are those truthful servants of Allah ﷻ who were sent with a new shariah and were given a new kitaab. It is not necessary for a Nabi to be given a new kitaab and a new shari'ah. It is possible that he followed the previous shari'ah and kitaab. There were many Nabis and Rasools who came to the dunya (world). Hadhrat Aadam عليه السلام was the first and our Nabi Hadhrat Muhammad Mustapha ﷺ was the last.

It is necessary for us to believe that all the Nabis and Rasools whom Allah ﷻ sent were true and our Nabi ﷺ is the greatest of all the Ambiyya.

The period of Nabi's ﷺ nubuwat

In the knowledge of Allah ﷻ, Nabi ﷺ received nubuwat before all the other Ambiyaa. However, in this world, Nabi ﷺ received nubuwat at the age of forty years and one day according to the lunar calendar.

Nabi ﷺ mentions: "I was in the cave of Hira when Jibraeel عليه السلام came to me and said, 'اِقْرَأ (read)'. I told him that I do not know how to read. Jibraeel عليه السلام then squeezed me very tightly and told me: 'Read.' Again I told him that I could not read. He then squeezed me for the second time and told me to read. Again I told him that I could not read. Jibraeel عليه السلام

8

then squeezed me for the third time and again asked me to read. I then asked him what should I read. At that time Jibraeel ﷺ recited the aayaat (verses) of Surah Iqra: اقْرَأْ بِاسْمِ رَبِّكَ الَّذِىْ خَلَقَ up to مَا لَمْ يَعْلَمْ." This was the first revelation received by Rasulullah ﷺ.

The beginning of tableegh (preaching)

Nabi ﷺ preached for three years in secret after receiving nubuwat. During this period thirty people accepted Islaam. Nabi ﷺ taught them in a house on the outskirts of Makkah. They also worshipped Allah ﷺ in this house.

Public preaching of Islaam and its opposition

When Nabi ﷺ was commanded to preach Islaam in public, the first thing that Nabi ﷺ did was to gather his family members from the Quraish at Mount Safa. He then told them:

"I am presenting to you such a gift which no person had presented to his people. I have brought that which will grant you success in your Deen (religion) and dunya (world). I take an oath in the name of Allah ﷺ that He has sent me to the world as a Nabi."

The Quraish did not appreciate this and spoke very harshly to Nabi ﷺ and rebuked him. They began opposing him. The person who opposed Nabi ﷺ the most was his uncle, Abu Lahab, regarding whom Surah Lahab was revealed. Nabi ﷺ did not worry about his opposition in any way and continued inviting the people to the straight path. The disbelievers caused such great difficulties and hardships to Nabi ﷺ and to the Sahaabah ﷺ, that listening to it will make the hair on one's body stand.

When Nabi ﷺ performed Salaah in the Ka`bah, the disbelivers tied a cloth around his mubaarak neck and pulled it. This would cause him to suffocate and his eyes would bulge out. At times the intestine's of a camel which was full of impurity was placed on his head. They even planned to smash Nabi's 鑾 mubaarak head and make him a shaheed (martyr). They threw stones at him. They stood on guard to ensure that nobody visited Nabi 鑾.

They inflicted severe punishments on the companions 鑾 of Rasulullah 鑾. The Sahaabah 鑾 were placed on burning hot coals. They were made to lie naked on the scorching hot desert sand and a boulder would be placed on them. They would be lashed throughout the night and during the day a rope would be tied around their necks and they were then dragged on the rocky grounds. Some of them used to be locked up in a room where they were made to inhale the smoke of a fire so that they could not breathe. Some of them were wrapped in animal skins and placed in the scorching sun. Some were tied to two camels and the camels were driven to run in opposite directions. When the camels ran, the bodies of the victims split in two. Hadhrat Sumayya رضي الله عنها was stabbed in her most sensitive part of her body and was killed in this manner.

Nabi 鑾 and his Sahaabah 鑾 were boycotted for three years. The disbelievers made every effort not to allow even a morsel of food or a sip of water to reach these Sahaabah 鑾 who believed in Allah 鑾. The children cried out of hunger but these oppressors never felt any pity for them. Their only crime was that they believed in Allah 鑾 and were not worshipping the stones that these disbelievers were worshipping. They did not join them in their theft, drinking, gambling, shameless and evil actions.

When the kuffar of Makkah could not achieve their objective of stopping Rasulullah 鑾 from making Tableegh-e-Deen (spreading the word of Deen), through oppression and persecution, they then decided to distract him with wealth and position.

They told him: "If you desire wealth we will grant you abundant wealth. If you desire leadership, we will appoint you as our king. If you wish to marry, we will marry you to the woman of your choice."

Nabi ﷺ had one answer: "I do not desire any of that. I cannot stop that Mission which I was sent with. If you place the sun in my one hand and the moon in the other, then too I will not abandon this work."

In short, the call towards the truth continued under every trying condition. Up to this day no power on earth can stop it. The opposing parties were destroyed and disgraced. Until Qiyaamah it will continue in this manner. So long as we stay firm on the path of Islaam and continue practising upon the teachings of our beloved Nabi ﷺ, we will never be overcome.

Hijrat (Migration)

The mushrikeen witnessing the progress of Islaam, collectively decided that they would harm the Muslims in every possible way. Since the king of Ethiopia was a just ruler, Nabi ﷺ permitted his Sahaabah ﵁ to migrate to Habsha (Ethiopia) so that they may worship Allah ﷻ with ease. Hence, on the 5th Rajab in the fifth year after nubuwat, fifteen or sixteen Sahaabah ﵁ migrated to Ethiopia. There were ten or eleven men and four or five women.

Failed attempts of the disbelievers

When the disbelievers heard of the Muslims migrating to Ethiopia, they followed the Muslims. A'mr ibnul A'as and Abdullah bin Umayyah were sent with many gifts to the king of Ethiopia. Through the medium of the priests they presented the gifts to the king and said:

"These people who have come to your land, have rebelled against their people. They will cause corruption. You should dismiss them from the land and hand them over to us."

The king replied:

"How can I hand them over to you without investigating this matter? This will cause me disgrace."

Thereafter, the king called the Muslims and enquired about their reasons for migrating. Hadhrat Ja'far ؓ went forward and delivered a very inspiring speech. The summary of his message is as follows:

"Most honourable king! We were a misguided nation who worshipped idols carved from stone. We lived on haraam (unlawful) earnings and carrion (dead animals). We would fight, kill, oppress and steal from one another. Corruption and evil became part of our lives. In order to reform us, Allah ﷻ sent us a messenger, whose nobility and lineage is known to all. His truthfulness and trustworthiness is famous among the Arabs. He called us to worship one God and saved us from worshipping idols. He commanded us to speak the truth, shun lying, deal with others respectfully, be kind to others, stay away from haraam (unlawful), not to harm others, not to use the wealth of orphans, be kind to widows, perform salaah, perform hajj and discharge our zakah. Your majesty, we believed him and brought Imaan on him."

He thereafter recited some aayaat (verses) of Surah Maryam and explained the belief of the Muslims regarding Hadhrat Maryam (alayhas salaam) and I'sa ؑ.

This truthful and inspiring talk affected the king so much that he accepted Islaam. He refused to handover the Muslims to the Quraish. The king's name was Ashamah. He was known as Najashi and was previously a Christian.

Second hijrat (migration) to Habsha (Ethiopia)

The Muslims were at ease in Habsha. They lived peacefully and were free to make the i'badat of Allah ﷻ. Upon receiving the news that the people of Makkah accepted Islaam, they returned to Makkah. On reaching Makkah they realised that the news was false. The disbelievers of Makkah were now even more oppressive against the believers. Therefore, Nabi ﷺ permitted the Muslims in the 7th year of nubuwat to migrate again to Habsha.

On this occasion, eighty-three men and eighteen women migrated. Besides them, other Yemeni Muslims, from the tribe of Hadhrat Abu Moosa Ash'ari ؓ, joined them.

Journey to Taa-if

There was nobody to assist Nabi ﷺ in Makkah after his uncle Abu Taalib died. The wife of Nabi ﷺ, Hadhrat Khadijah رضي الله عنها, who was a source of great comfort to him had also passed away. In the meantime, the people of Makkah increased their oppression and persecution of the Muslims worsened.

Having thus lost hope in the people of Makkah, Nabi ﷺ decided to travel to Taa-if, thinking that it was a town of honourable people. If they accepted Islaam it would have a good effect. Hence, in the 10th year of Nubuwat, Nabi ﷺ and Hadhrat Zaid bin Haaritha ؓ set out for Taa-if.

On reaching Taa-if, Nabi ﷺ spoke to the leaders and invited them to Islaam. Contrary to his expectations, they dealt with him very harshly. They insulted and jeered him, set evil people behind him to stone him, due to which Nabi ﷺ began to bleed. When Nabi ﷺ sat down for a while, these wretched people chased him and started pelting him with stones again. Hadhrat Zaid bin Haaritha ؓ, who was protecting Nabi ﷺ, was also injured.

Whilst returning from Taa-if, Nabi ﷺ rested in an orchard where he made a very fervent dua. The owner of the orchard felt sorry for Nabi ﷺ and sent his slave, whose name was A'ddaas, with some khajoor (dates). Before eating the dates, Nabi ﷺ recited *bismillah*. A'ddaas who was a Christian commented: "There is nobody in this area who takes this name."

Nabi ﷺ asked him where he came from?" He replied: "I am from Neenway." Nabi ﷺ asked him: "Is it the same Neenway where a pious servant of Allah ﷻ by the name of Yunus ibn Matta lived?" A'ddaas replied: "How do you know about him?" Nabi ﷺ replied: "He was a Nabi and I am also a Nabi."

On hearing this A'ddaas kissed the forehead and hands of Nabi ﷺ and accepted Islaam. When A'ddaas ؓ returned, his master asked him: "What were you doing? This person could misguide you." A'ddaas ؓ replied: "He is the final Prophet. All the Ambiyaa of the past have given glad tidings about him."

As Nabi ﷺ continued, Hadhrat Jibraeel السلام عليه appeared at a place called Qarn-uth-Tha'alib and said: "Allah ﷻ knows very well how the people have treated you and He has sent an angel who is in charge of the mountains to assist you in whatever you wish."

The angel came to Nabi ﷺ and after making salaam said: "If you order me I will crush the people between these two mountains." Nabi ﷺ replied: "No. I have hope in Allah ﷻ that their progeny will worship Allah ﷻ and they will not ascribe any partners to Him."

Subsequently, this is exactly what happened and all the people of Taa-if became Muslims.

Mi'raaj

The incident of Mi'raaj took place after returning from Taa-if in the tenth year after nubuwat. The occasion of Mi'raaj has great significance in Islaamic history. From amongst all the Ambiyaa, this honour of Mi'raaj was granted only to our Nabi ﷺ.

A brief explanation of this incident is as follows:

Jibraeel عليه السلام and Mikaaeel عليه السلام seated Nabi ﷺ on the buraaq (a special horse from Jannah) and took him from Makkah to Musjid-ul-Aqsa in Jerusalem. This buraaq was very swift. The length of each step was as far as one could see. When they reached Musjid-ul-Aqsa, adhaan was called out and Nabi ﷺ lead the Salaah whilst all the other Ambiyaa followed.

Thereafter, Nabi ﷺ ascended the different skies where he met the different Ambiyaa عليه السلام. On the first sky he met Aadam عليه السلام, on the second sky I'sa عليه السلام and Yahya عليه السلام, on the third sky Yusuf عليه السلام, on the fourth sky Idrees عليه السلام, on the fifth sky Haroon عليه السلام, on the sixth sky Moosa عليه السلام and on the seventh sky he met Ebrahim عليه السلام. (Saheeh Al-Bukhaari)

Thereafter, Nabi ﷺ went to the Sidrat-ul-Muntaha (a point very close to the A'rsh [throne of Allah ﷻ] beyond which no creation can pass) and entered Jannah. There he saw the wonders of Jannah. Nabi ﷺ then saw Jahannum, which was filled with different types of punishments. Nabi ﷺ went further and was given the ultimate hounour of being in the presence of Allah ﷻ.

In reality, Rasulullah ﷺ did not only experience a spiritual encounter with Allah ﷻ, but was also given the highest honour of being in the presence of Allah ﷻ, seeing Him with his physical eyes and also communicating with Him. It was on this occassion that salaah was made fardh (compulsory). Thereafter, Nabi ﷺ returned to Makkah. This entire journey took place in just one night.

The next morning the news of the Mi'raaj spread in Makkah and people began mocking Nabi ﷺ. To test Nabi ﷺ they asked him to describe Baitul Maqdis and his other experiences. Nabi ﷺ gave a clear description of all that they enquired of him.

On his return, Nabi ﷺ passed by the trade caravans of the Quraish, which were on their way to Shaam at that time. He greeted them and they recognised the voice of Nabi ﷺ. When these caravans returned to Makkah they bore testimony to this and other incidents they had witnessed. These were clear proofs for those who refused to believe him. Even with proof, the disbelievers eventually began saying that this journey was an act of sorcery and that Nabi ﷺ was a magician.

The believers, on the other hand, accepted the Mi'raaj without any doubt. The first to accept it was Hadhrat Abu Bakr Siddeeq ﷺ.

Lessons of Mi'raaj

A group of people with fingernails of copper were scratching their faces and chests. When Nabi ﷺ enquired about this group, Jibraeel عليه السلام replied that they were those who made gheebat (used to backbite) in the world.

One person was swimming in a river and a boulder was being thrown at him continuously. When Jibraeel عليه السلام was asked who this person was, he replied that he used to deal in interest.

There was a group of people whose heads were being smashed by boulders. Thereafter their heads would return to their original form and get smashed again. This punishment continued all the time. When Nabi ﷺ asked Jibraeel عليه السلام who these people were, he replied that they were those who did not perform their fardh salaah.

A group of people had rags tied around their private parts. They were grazing on the thorns and stones of Jahannum as camels graze. Jibraeel عليه السلام explained that they were those who did not pay their zakah.

16

Some men and women were in front of two pots. One pot had cooked meat and the other had rotten meat. They were eating the rotten meat. Nabi 襲 asked Jibraeel عليه السلام who they were. He replied that they were those men and women who committed zina (adultery).

There was a stick that was in the middle of a path. It would tear up whoever passed by it. When Nabi 襲 asked Jibraeel عليه السلام about this, he replied that this is the example of those ummatis (followers) who hide on the side of the roads and loot the people passing by (highway robbers).

A group of people collected a huge pile of wood. which they were unable to carry, yet they continued adding to the pile of wood. Hadhrat Jibraeel عليه السلام explained that this is the example of those who despite having not fulfilled the trusts rights of people, yet they continue to burden themselves with more responsibilities.

The tongues and lips of a group of people were being cut with iron scissors. After being cut, they would return to normal. Their tongues and lips would then be cut again and in this manner the punishment continued. When Jibraeel عليه السلام was asked who they were, he replied that these were the people who would deliver lectures and advise others, but they themselves did not practise upon it.

Islaam in Madinah Munawwarah

Nabi ﷺ continued preaching Islaam among the people after receiving the responsibility of Nubuwat. He would go alone to the market places and meet the people. He made every possible effort. Despite this, with the exception of a few, the people mocked at him and caused all types of difficulties to him.

Ten years passed in this relentless effort. During this period, some people from the tribe of Khazraj of Madinah came to Makkah and met Nabi ﷺ. Among them were two men, one by the name of As'ad bin Zuraarah and the other by the name of Zakwaan bin A'bdil Qais. Six or eight men in that group accepted Islaam. As'ad ؓ and Zakwaan ؓ were among them.

Nabi ﷺ asked them: "Will you assist me in preaching Islaam?" They replied: "Presently we are engaged in war. It will be inappropriate for you to come to Madinah now. It will be better if Nabi ﷺ comes when peace has been restored. We will make an effort for now and return the next year."

They went back to Madinah and began making an effort for peace. The fight between the Ows and Khazraj ended. Keeping to their promise, the group returned the next year at the time of haj. Among them were ten people from the Khazraj and two from the Ows. In this group those who had not become Muslims the previous year now accepted Islaam. This bay'at (promise) with Nabi ﷺ took place in a valley and is known as Bay'at-ul-A`qabah-Al-Ula.

When these people returned to Madinah and started making tabligh (spreading Islaam), Islaam began to be discussed in every home. This "New Deen" became the main topic of discussion in the whole of Madinah.

First Madrasah in Madinah Munawwarah

The Ows and Khazraj together addressed a letter to Nabi 變, which stated: *"Al-hamdulillah!* The propagation of Islaam has been established in Madinah. Please send someone who will teach us the Qur'aan, teach us the Deen, and assist us in further propagating and establisihing Deen-e-Islaam"

Nabi 變 chose Hadhrat Mus'ab bin 'Umair ﷺ for this work and sent him to Madinah Munawwarah. When he reached Madinah, he started a madrasah and began working with the people. After making an effort for only one year, he sent a group of seventy men and two women to Nabi 變 the following year at the time of haj.

Nabi 變 hosted them warmly and at night spoke to them for a long time in a valley. Each one of them took bay'at (promise) at the hands of Nabi 變 that they will remain steadfast on his teachings at all times and they will assist Nabi 變 in his efforts.

They then asked: "What will we receive in exchange?" Nabi 變 replied: "The pleasure of Allah 變 and Jannah." On hearing this they all said that they were happy and pleased with this.

History is proof to the fact that these people fulfilled this promise until their deaths. Their children also remained steadfast to it. This bay't promise) is known as Bay't-ul-A'qabah Ath-thaaniyah (the second pledge of A'qbah).

Hijrat (migration) to Madinah Munawwarah

When the people of Makkah heard that the people of Madinah had taken bay't (a promise) at the hands of Nabi 卿, their anger knew no bounds. Every day they thought of new plans to harm the Muslims.

Seeing this condition, Nabi 卿 suggested to the Sahaabah 鑻 to make hijrat (migrate) to Madinah Munawwarah. The Sahaabah 鑻 secretly left for Madinah until there were no Muslims left in Makkah besides Nabi 卿, Hadhrat Abu Bakr 鑻, Hadhrat Ali 鑻 and a few weak Sahaabah 鑻. Hadhrat Abu Bakr 鑻 also intended to migrate but Nabi 卿 stopped him and told him to wait a while and make hijrat with him.

Hadhrat Abu Bakr 鑻 was waiting to make hijrat and set aside two camels for this journey, one for himself and the other for Nabi 卿.

The disbelievers were constantly making effort to harm the Muslims, each one taking a part. One day they gathered at Darun-Nadwa to decide what course of action should be adopted against Nabi 卿. Some suggested that he should be imprisoned. Some suggested that he should be banished. The cunning and evil ones among them did not accept these ideas and said that they would not be successful by doing this.

Abu Jahl suggested that Nabi 卿 should be killed. One person from each tribe should take part in this so that Nabi's 卿 family would not be able to take revenge.

Allah 謎 informed Nabi 卿 of this meeting and at once Nabi 卿 decided to make hijrat. At night he told Hadhrat Ali 鑻 to sleep in his bed. The amaanaat (trusts) of the non-muslims that were kept by Nabi 卿 were all handed over to Hadhrat Ali 鑻 with the instruction to return them to the people the next morning.

Thereafter, when Nabi 卿 left his home, he saw a group of the disbelievers waiting at the door. Nabi 卿 came out of the house reciting Surah Yaseen and when he reached the ayat (verse):

$$\text{فَأَغْشَيْنَاهُمْ فَهُمْ لاَ يُبْصِرُوْن}$$

And We have enveloped (with the darkness of Kufr and sin) them so they cannot see (the truth)

He repeated it several times. Due to this, Allah ﷻ blinded the disbelievers and they were unable to see Nabi ﷺ emerge from his home.

Nabi ﷺ then went to the house of Hadhrat Abu Bakr ؓ and found him waiting there. Hadhrat Abu Bakr ؓ had engaged a guide to show them the way. They left his house from the back and went towards Mount Thaur.

The cave of Thaur

At night Nabi ﷺ and Hadhrat Abu Bakr ؓ left Makkah and went towards the cave of Thaur. When the disbelievers came to know the next morning that Nabi ﷺ had left his home, they became very worried and sent people to search for him. Those who were experts in *qiyaafah*, an art of tracking footprints, followed the footprints of Nabi ﷺ and came to the cave. If they bent a little, they would have seen Nabi ﷺ. Hadhrat Abu Bakr ؓ became very worried but Nabi ﷺ consoled him saying: "Do not fear. Allah ﷻ is with us." Allah ﷻ caused the disbelievers to turn away from the cave without looking inside.

Umayyah bin Khalaf said: "How could anyone enter this cave? A spider has spun its web over the entrance and a pigeon has built its nest and laid its eggs at the entrance."

This was the plan of Allah ﷻ. When Allah ﷻ wishes to safeguard a person, He creates the means for it. Nabi ﷺ and Hadhrat Abu Bakr ؓ remained in this cave for three days until the disbelievers lost hope in finding them.

During these three days Hadhrat Abu Bakr's ؓ son Abdullah used to bring news from Makkah at night and would return before the morning. His daughter, Hadhrat Asma رضي الله عنها, would send food for them. Abdullah commanded his slave to herd the sheep up to the cave so that Nabi ﷺ and Hadhrat Abu Bakr ؓ footprints would be erased and the disbelievers of Makkah would not be able to track them

Journey to Madinah Munawwarah

After staying for three days in the cave of Thaur, Hadhrat Abu Bakr's ؓ slave, A'amir bin Fuhayrah ؓ brought both the camels to the cave on monday the 4th of Rabi-ul-Awwal. He also brought the guide whose name was Abdullah-bin-Urayqit.

The unseen help of Allah ﷻ

Nabi ﷺ left the cave of Thaur with Hadhrat Abu Bakr ؓ, A'amir bin Fuhayrah ؓ and Abdullah bin Urayqit. At the same time Suraaqah bin Maalik was sent by the Quraish in search of Nabi ﷺ. As he approached Nabi ﷺ, his horse slipped and he fell off. He then climbed back on to his horse and followed Nabi ﷺ.

Hadhrat Abu Bakr ؓ turned around and looked at him but Nabi ﷺ did not pay any attention to him. When Suraaqah came very close, the legs of his horse sunk into the ground up to its knees and Suraaqah fell off for the second time. He tried to pull out the horse's legs but was unable to do so. Having found himself in this predicament, he was forced to ask Nabi ﷺ for protection and Nabi ﷺ granted him safety.

Through the *barakah* (blessings) of Nabi ﷺ, his horse was freed. When the horse's legs came out of the ground, smoke began to rise from that spot. When Suraaqah saw this, he took a warning from it. With extreme humility he presented some of his provisions to Nabi ﷺ which Nabi ﷺ did not accept. He only requested Suraaqah not tell anyone of his whereabouts. Suraaqah fulfilled this promise and only after a few days narrated this incident to Abu Jahl and advised him not to oppose Nabi ﷺ.

Mu'jizah (miracle) of Nabi ﷺ

On the way to Madinah Munawwarah, Nabi ﷺ passed by the tent of Umme Ma`bad. A goat, that was not giving milk, was tied at one side of her tent. Nabi ﷺ sought her permission and passed his hands over its udders. The udders filled with milk to such an extent, that Nabi ﷺ and all his companions ؓ drank from it. Thereafter, they continued on the journey. When Umme Ma'bad's husband returned and heard what had occurred, he exclaimed: "By the qasam of Allah ﷻ! This is the very same pious person from Makkah."

Thereafter, both of them made hijrat to Madinah Munawwarah and accepted Islaam.

Stay in Quba and the beginning of the Islaamic calendar

Before entering Madinah Munawwarah, Nabi ﷺ stayed for fourteen days on the outskirts in Quba. It was here that he built the first Musjid in the history of Islaam.

Before making hijrat, Nabi ﷺ entrusted the amanaat (trusts) that people had left with him, to Hadhrat Ali ؓ. Hadhrat Ali ؓ returned these amanaat (trusts) to their owners in Makkah. Thereafter, he left for Madinah Munawwarah and joined Nabi ﷺ in Quba.

Hadhrat Umar ؓ subsequently started the Islaamic calendar from the time of hijrat. The first month of the Islaamic calendar was fixed as Muharram.

Entrance into Madinah Munawwarah

Nabi 🌺 prepared to leave for Madinah on a Friday in the month of Rabi-ul-Awwal. The Ansaar of Madinah were walking alongside the camel of Nabi 🌺. They were full of joy and the young children recited poetry. They reached the area of the Banu Saalim at the time of Jumuah. Nabi 🌺 performed the Jumuah Salaah at that place. After the Salaah, Nabi 🌺 climbed back onto the animal and proceeded to Madinah.

Whenever Nabi 🌺 passed the house of an Ansaari, he would request Nabi 🌺 to stay at his home. Nabi 🌺 would reply: "Leave the camel to its destination. Wherever Allah 🌺 wills, it will stop."

The camel continued walking and finally sat in front of the house of Hadhrat Abu Ayyub Ansaari 🌺. Nabi 🌺 thereafter stayed at Hadhrat Abu Ayyub Ansaari 🌺 house.

Construction of Musjid-un-Nabawi

There was no Musjid in Madinah Munawwarah before the arrival of Nabi 🌺. The place where the camel of Nabi 🌺 sat was purchased and the Musjid was built at that spot. The walls were built from unbaked bricks, the pillars were made from date palms and the roof was made from its branches.

It appears in some narrations that stones were placed as walls and thereafter in every era changes and alterations were made to the Musjid until the present age as we see it. May Allah 🌺 allow those people, who keep the Musjid occupied, to flourish till the Day of Qiyaamah. Aameen.

There were two apartments built with the Musjid. One was for Hadhrat Aaishah رضي الله عنها and the other for Hadhrat Sowda رضي الله عنها. After these two houses, more apartments were built according to the need.

Mu-aakhaat (Brotherhood)

Those Sahaabah ﷺ who came from Makkah to Madinah were totally destitute. Nabi ﷺ made the Muhajireen and Ansaar enter into an agreement of brotherhood to support and assist each other. The Ansaar would compete with one another in offering assistance to the Muhaajireen. They allowed the Muhaajireen to do as they felt with their houses, wealth, properties and orchards and gave preference to the Muhaajireen over themselves.

Once an Ansaari sahaabi told his Muhaajir brother to take half of his wealth. "My house has two sections," he said. "Take whichever section you wish. I have two wives. I will divorce the one you like and you can marry her thereafter."

The Muhaajir sahaabi replied: "May Allah ﷻ bless you in your wealth and family. Show me the way to the marketplace and I will see to my own needs."

In short, the Ansaar displayed great support and the Muhaajireen displayed the highest form of independence. If a Muhaajir did take anything, he made up for it later. They initially also inherited from each other due to mu-aakhaat (brotherhood), but later Allah ﷻ cancelled this law when the ayaat of inheritance were revealed.

Treaty with the Jews

The Jews of Madinah knew very well that Nabi ﷺ was the final Prophet and that the Ambiyaa عليهم السلام of the past had given glad tidings regarding him. However, due to their hatred and enmity for Nabi ﷺ, they continued opposing him and plotting with the disbelievers of Makkah against him.

After Nabi ﷺ settled in Madinah, their enmity increased. They realised that they would no longer be respected and honoured in the presence of

Nabi 🕮. With the exception of a few Jews who embraced Islaam, the rest of them were burning with jealousy and hatred for him.

Nabi 🕮 felt it necessary to enter into a treaty with them in order to be safe from their mischief. The treaty included the following:

1. The Jews would be free to practise their religion.
2. If the Muslims or Jews engaged in war, each would render assistance to the other.
3. The Jews and Muslims will maintain friendly relationships.
4. In the event of an attack on Madinah, the Muslims and Jews will join forces.
5. If either of them enters into a treaty with an enemy, the other group would also recognise the treaty.
6. None of the groups will side with the Quraish.
7. If the Muslims engaged in war against anyone, the Jews would assist in the expenses.
8. The oppressed would be given assistance.
9. If a dispute occurred between the Muslims and the Jews, the responsibility of settlement would rest with Nabi 🕮.

The Jews did not adhere to this treaty. In the 2nd year, the Banu Qaynuqaa' broke the treaty. Likewise the Banu Nadheer broke the treaty in the 4th year and the Banu Quraizah in the 5th year.

Adhaan

Nabi 🕮 disliked using the methods of the Jews and Christians for calling the people to assemble at the time of Salaah. There was a need to adopt a method to gather the people in the Musjid at the time of Salaah. Allah 🕮 showed some of the Sahaabah 🕮 the adhaan in their dreams. The Sahaabah 🕮 related their dreams to Nabi 🕮 and he accepted the adhaan as the method of gathering people to the Musjid. It was then introduced and implemented in the shariah. Hadhrat Bilal 🕮 was appointed as the muadh-dhin and Allah 🕮 made him the leader of the muadh-dhins till the Day of Qiyaamah.

Jihaad

During Nabi's ﷺ stay in Makkah till the age of fifty three, he continued inviting people to Islaam with softness and gentleness. He went to each home, the market places and the different tribes explaining to them about Islaam. The suffering and hardship that Nabi ﷺ and his Sahaabah ؓ underwent was never witnessed before in history and it will never be witnessed in the future. Despite all these hardships, Nabi ﷺ encouraged his followers to be patient and never allowed thoughts of revenge to be considered by the Muslims.

Nabi ﷺ and his Sahaabah ؓ were forced to leave their hometown leaving behind their wealth and properties, which fell into the ownership of the disbelievers. This period of extreme suffering and loss, trial and tribulation, was borne by Allah's Rasul ﷺ and his beloved Sahaabah with tolerance, is forever recorded in History. The Kuffar of Makkah did not end their acts of tyranny and oppression but continued in their evil ways by agitating the Jews and Non-Muslim tribes around Madinah against the Muslims. Their primary objective was to completely eradicate Islaam and destroy the Muslims.

Allah ﷻ finally instructed Nabi ﷺ to engage in jihaad. The objective was neither to cause disorder and bloodshed nor to oppress others or force them to accept Islaam. In fact, Islaam prohibits forceful conversions into Islaam. Allah ﷻ states in the Qur'aan:

لَاۤ اِكْرَاهَ فِى الدِّيْن

"There is no compulsion to enter into Islaam"

The real purpose of jihaad is to remove the dangers and corruption of those who are an obstacle in the path of the servants of Allah ﷻ who promote the kalimah, practise on the commands of Allah ﷻ and invite others towards it. Jihaad is waged primarily against those who obstruct the establishment of Islaam and are a danger and hinderance to those who are engaged in this honourable duty. Instead, if non-Muslims live in a Muslim country peacefully, Islaam grants protection to them in their lives, wealth, property and honour. This is the purpose of jihaad. There are also other benefits of jihaad:

- The oppressed people are saved from oppressive rulers.
- Those who cannot accept Islaam due to fear of oppressive rulers will be free to accept Islaam.
- Islaam and Muslims who are overwhelmed and oppressed can be saved from the harms of their enemies and adversaries.
- The disbelievers will develop an awe for the Muslims. In effect, this will save the Muslims from the mischief of the kuffaar.

Did Islaam spread by the sword?

History is witness to the manner in which Rasulullah ﷺ preached Islaam and in what conditions he had done so. Did Nabi ﷺ ever take a sword and harshly force the people to accept Islaam? It is clear that Nabi ﷺ never preached Islaam by force.

How was it possible for such a person to have spread Islaam by force when his background was as follows:

- He was an orphan even before he was born.
- He lost his mother at a tender age.
- He shifted from the care of one person to another during his childhood.
- He lived his entire life in a state of destitution.
- A fire was not lit for months on end in his home.
- His own family became his enemies because he preached the truth.
- He was unable to find a place of refuge for himself and for his friends in a city that granted peace and security to the entire creation.

Is it possible to imagine such a person using force to convert people towards his own ideologies?

Even after this state of helplessness, when Islaam gained strength and many brave and powerful people entered the fold of Islaam, no Muslim raised a finger against the disbelievers. Instead, the Muslims continued tolerating all sorts of oppression inflicted on them by their enemies.

The teachings of Islaam have a special kind of appeal and attraction. It advocates kindness to the creation and terminates oppression and tyranny. It implements justice and fairness and it grants protection to the life, honour and wealth of every individual.

These beautiful qualities of the Muslims attracted people and they accepted Islaam willingly and wholeheartedly. They were then prepared to sacrifice themselves for the cause of Islaam.

Unfortunately today, the Muslims have become unmindful of these beautiful qualities, due to which they themselves are being disgraced and have also become an obstacle for others entering into the fold of Islaam.

The status of jihaad

In Islaam, the institution of jihaad is *fardh* (compulsory). However, according to different circumstances, jihaad is either *fardh-e-a`in* (compulsory on every person) or at times *fardh-e-kifaayah* (compulsory on a group of people who will be able to carry it out). At times the injunction of *jihaad-bis-saif* (fighting) is applicable and at times the command of *jihaad-bil-maal* (donating and spending) is applicable. It also happens that certain people are given the command of *jihaad-bis-saif* and certain people are given the command of *jihaad-bil-maal*. On occasions it becomes necessary to defend the Islamic cause either through literature or lectures and oration. When such occasions arise, it will become fardh to engage in these activities.

Ghazwah, Jaish and Sariyyah

Ghazwah is a battle in which Nabi ﷺ participated. The battle in which Nabi ﷺ did not participate and where the army was large is called a Jaish. If the army was small, it was called Sariyyah.

Nabi ﷺ participated in twenty-three Ghazawaat. Some say it was twenty-seven. Fighting took place in nine of them. These are as follows:

1. The First Battle of Badr
2. The Second Battle of Badr
3. The Battle of Uhud
4. The Battle of Ahzaab
5. The Battle of Banu Quraizah
6. The Battle of Ban-ul-Mustalaq
7. The Battle of Khaibar
8. The Battle of Hunain
9. The Battle of Taa-if

The Muslims were victorious in all these wars. However, in the Battle of Uhud, the Muslims gained victory at first, but due to the mistake of some Muslims they were temporarily defeated. In the Battle of Hunain some Muslims suffered a temporary defeat but Allah ﷺ thereafter granted them victory. In the battles besides these nine, the enemy either entered into a treaty with the Muslims or some incident occurred whereby the enemy was over-awed and unable to fight.

Ghazawaat and Sarayaa

Hadhrat Mufti Shafee` Sahib ﷦ has drawn a table of all the ghazawaat and sarayaa in his kitab Seerat Khaatam-ul-Ambiyaa. The table is as follows:

Year	Ghazwah	Sariyyah
		Under the command of;
1 A.H.	None	(1) Hamzah ﷺ (2) U`baidah ﷺ
2 A.H.	(1) Abwaa / Duwaan (2) Buwaat (3) Badr(most significant battle of the year) (4) Banu Qaynuqaa` (5) Saweeq	(3) Abdullah bin Jahsh ﷺ (4) U`mair (5) Saalim
3 A.H.	(6) Ghatfaan (7) Uhud (most significant battle of the year) (8) Hamraa-ul-Asad	(6) Muhammad bin Maslamah ﷺ towards Qurtaa (7) Zaid bin Haaritha ﷺ
4 A.H.	(9) Banu Nadheer (10) BadrSughra	(8) Abu Salimah (9) Abdullah bin Unais (10) Munzir (11) Marthad
5 A.H.	(11) Zat-ur-Riqaa` (12) Doomat-ul-Jandal (13) Muraisee` / Banul- Mustaliq (14) Khandaq (most significant battle of the year)	None
6 A.H.	(15) Banu Lihyaan (16) Ghabah / Zi Qarad (17) Hudaybiyyah	(12) Muhammad bin Maslamah ﷺ towards Zil Qassah (13) Zaid bin Haarithah ﷺ towards Bani Sulaim (14) Abdurrahman bin Auf ﷺ (15) Ali ﷺ (16) Zaid bin Haarithah ﷺ

		towards Ummu Qirfah (17) Abdullah bin 'Ateek (18) Abdullah bin Rawahah ؓ (19) Kuraz bin Jaabir (20) A'mr Dhamiri (21) U'kashah (22) Muhammad bin Maslamah ؓ towards Qurtaa
7 A.H.	(18) Khaibar *(most significant battle for the year)*	(23) Abu Bakr ؓ (24) Bishr bin Sa`d (25) Ghaalib bin Abdullah (26) Basheer (27) Akhram
8 A.H.	(19) Fath-e-Makkah (20) Hunain (21) Taaif	(28) Muta (29) Ghaalib – towards Banul-Mulawwih (30) Ghaalib – towards Fadak (31) Shujaa' (32) Ka'b (33) A'mr bin A'as ؓ (34) Abu Ubaidah bin Jarrah ؓ (35) Abu Qataadah (36) Khaalid / Ghumaisa (37) Tufail bin A'mr Dowsi (38) Qutbah
9 A.H.	(22) Tabuk *(amongst the significant battles)*	(39) Alqamah (40) Ali ؓ (41) U`kashah
10 A.H.	None (Hajja-tul-Widaa' performed this year)	(42) Khaalid bin Waleed ؓ towards Najraan (43) Ali ؓ towards Yemen
11 A.H.	None	(44) Nabi ﷺ commanded that the Sariyyah of Usamah ؓ be sent but they only left after the demise of Nabi ﷺ.

Important Ghazawaat, Sarayaa and events

The year 1 A.H. (After Hijri)

Sariyyah of Hamzah and Sariyyah of U'baidah bin Haarith ؓ

Seven months after hijrat in the month of Ramadhaan, Nabi ﷺ sent Hadhrat Hamzah ؓ and a group of Sahaabah ؓ with a white flag towards a Quraishi caravan. There was a short encounter but Majdiy bin A`mr intervened and stopped the fight.

In Shawwaal Hadhrat U`baidah ؓ was made the Ameer of sixty Sahaabah ؓ and sent towards Batnur Rabigh to confront Abu Sufyaan. It was in this jihaad that Hadhrat Sa'd bin Abi Waqqaas ؓ shot the first arrow against the disbelievers.

In this year Al-Musjid-un-Nabawi ﷺ was built and the adhaan was introduced.

33

The year 2 A.H.

Changing of the Qiblah

In this year the injunction to face the Ka`bah, instead of facing Bait-ul-Maqdis as the Qiblah in salaah was received as wahee.

Sariyyah of Abdullah bin Jahsh 🌸 and the first booty in Islaam

In the month of Rajab, Nabi 🌸 appointed Hadhrat Abdullah bin Jahsh 🌸 over twelve Sahaabah 🌸 and sent them to confront a Quraishi caravan. Coincidentally, the day the caravan approached them, was the first day of Rajab. In the beginning of Islaam it was prohibited to fight during this month. The Sahaabah 🌸 were under the impression that it was still the 30th of Jumad-uth-Thaani. Hence, after consulting with each another, they decided to attack the caravan.

They attacked the caravan and killed their leader. Two people were captured. The occupants of the caravan fled and left all their wealth, which fell in the hands of the Muslims as booty.

The Ameer, Hadhrat Abdullah bin Jahsh 🌸 distributed the booty among the Sahaabah 🌸 and kept one fifth of it for the bait-ul-maal (public treasury). It appears in some narrations that they brought all the booty to Nabi 🌸. Nabi 🌸 mentioned that he had not commanded the Sahaabah 🌸 to fight in the month of Rajab but as stated it was done in error. Nabi 🌸 retained this booty till the Battle of Badr and thereafter, distributed it with the booty from Badr.

This incident caused an uproar among the Arabs as the Muslims fought in the month of Rajab whereas it was prohibited to do so. The following Aayat was revealed in answer to this:

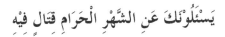

يَسْئَلُوْنَكَ عَنِ الشَّهْرِ الْحَرَامِ قِتَالٍ فِيْهِ

They ask you regarding the fighting in the sacred months.

The aayat explained that fighting in the sacred months is a prohibited act but the Muslims made a mistake. Those who raise objections should ponder over their own mischief and wrongdoings. For example, they:

(1) Prevented the people from exposure and acceptance of the Deen (religion) of Allah 𝕮.
(2) Ascribed partners with Allah 𝕮. (The gravest of sins).
(3) Prevented the people from making ibaadat of Allah 𝕮 in His house.
(4) Removed them from that city of Allah 𝕮 where safety is granted to everyone.

Such objectors who carry out the abovementioned acts were in fact committing crimes which were worse than fighting in the sacred months.

The Battle of Badr

The most significant battle fought in this year

Approximately eighty miles (128 km) from Madinah, there is a well called Badr. The village derived its name from this well. The battle of Badr was fought here.

The strength of the Quraish depended largely on trade. The profits earned through trade were used to fight the Muslims. It was decided that this pillar of strength should be weakened. There was a Quraishi caravan coming from Shaam (Syria) which Nabi 鱗 was informed of. He set out on the 12th Ramadhaan 2 A.H. with three hundred and thirteen Sahaabah 鱗 to confront this caravan. They reached *Rowhaa* which is forty miles (64km) to the south from Madinah and camped there. The leader of the Quraishi caravan heard of their plan and changed his route. He then sent a person with the message to the Quraish to prepare an army to assist him.

The Quraish had previously planned to attack the Muslims. When they received the news, they prepared an army of nine hundred and fifty youth. One hundred of them were on horseback. They had seven hundred camels. Many leaders of the Quraish and wealthy people joined this group.

Sacrifice of the Sahaabah 鱗

When Nabi 鱗 received this information, he consulted the Sahaabah 鱗. Hadhrat Abu Bakr 鱗 and other Sahaabah 鱗 offered their lives and wealth. U`mair bin Abi Waqqas 鱗 was a young lad at that time and because of his youth, Nabi 鱗 stopped him from taking part in jihaad. He began to cry. On seeing this, Nabi 鱗 granted him permission and he joined the Sahaabah 鱗.

Sa'd bin U'badah ⚘, the leader of the Ansaar, said: "By the qasam of Allah 🌼, if you command us to dive into the sea we will do so." He then delivered a very inspiring speech.

Hadhrat Miqdad ⚘ said: "O Rasulullah 🌼! We will fight on your right and your left and from all sides around you."

Nabi 🌼 became very pleased on hearing this and gave the order to advance. When they drew close to Badr, they realised that Abu Sufyaan had already reached Makkah with his trade caravan and a large army of the Quraish had camped on one corner of the field. Even after the trade caravan was out of danger, Abu Jahl insisted on fighting.

When the Muslim army heard of this, they went forward but the Quraish reached the battlefield before them and took control of all the spots that were advantageous for fighting. In this manner they tried to secure an upper hand. When the Muslims reached Badr, they were left with a sandy area which was not conducive for fighting. It was very difficult to even walk there and there was no sign of any water.

The unseen help of Allah 🌼

Allah's 🌼 assistance came to the Muslims in the form of rain. As a result, the sandy ground became firm and the entire army had drinking water for themselves and their animals. All of them filled their containers and had even built a pond to store the rain water. Due to the rain, the area that the disbelievers took control of became muddy and this made walking there difficult.

Muslims fulfilling their promises

The Muslims were very small in number and were in a defenceless position. An army of a thousand well-equipped youth were to face them. Even one person coming to their assistance in such a situation, was invaluable. However, in Islaam one has to keep to his promise.

A very interesting incident occurred which shows the integrity of a Muslim in keeping to his word. The incident regarding this promise is as follows:

Hadhrat Hudhaifah 鼇 and Hadhrat Khansa 鼇 were two Sahaabah who had set out to assist the Muslims. On the way the disbelievers confronted them, only allowing them to continue on the promise not to assist the Muslims in this jihaad. When Nabi 鼇 learnt of this he prevented them from participating in the jihaad and said: "We fulfil our promises at all times."

At the commencement of the battle, when the rows of both the armies were arranged, three warriors from the Quraish advanced. Hadhrat Ali 鼇, Hadhrat Hamzah 鼇 and Hadhrat U`baidah bin Haarith 鼇 proceeded from the Muslim army to combat them. All the three disbelievers were killed. From the three Muslims, only Hadhrat U`baidah 鼇 was wounded. Hadhrat Ali 鼇 lifted him on his shoulders and brought him to Nabi 鼇. Nabi 鼇 rested Hadhrat U`baidah's 鼇 face on his mubaarak leg and dusted his face. At that time Hadhrat U`baidah 鼇 was nearing his end and was about to pass away. He asked Nabi 鼇: "Will I be deprived of shahaadat (martyrdom)?" Nabi 鼇 replied: "No. You are a shaheed and I am a witness to it."

Hadhrat U'baidah 鼇 also recevied the great honour of Nabi 鼇 descending into his grave and burying him with his own mubaarak hands.

Thereafter, a fierce battle broke out. Rasulullah 薹 fell in sajdah and continued asking Allah 薹 for His assistance until eventually Nabi 薹 was given the glad tiding of victory.

Death of Abu Jahl

Abu Jahl's hatred for Islaam was known to one and all. Two Ansaari youngsters, Mu'aaz and Mu'awwiz 薹 made a pact that when they see Abu Jahl, they will kill him, or they themselves will be killed. However they did not know who he was. Hence they asked Hadhrat Abdurrahmaan bin A'uf 薹 as to who Abu Jahl was. He pointed out Abu Jahl. They both advanced like hawks and attacked him with their swords. They injured him and dropped him to the ground. Thereafter another sahaabi came and finished him off.

On seeing this, I'kramah the son of Abu Jahl (who was not yet a Muslim), came from behind and struck the shoulder of Mu`aaz 薹. This blow cut his shoulder. Mu'aaz 薹 experienced tremendous pain due to this. He placed his arm under his foot and severed it from his body. He then continued fighting. May Allah 薹 grant us all such enthusiasm.

A great miracle

By the command of Allah 薹, Nabi 薹 picked a handful of stones and flung it at the disbelievers. Nabi 薹 then instructed the Sahaabah 薹 to attack the enemy unexpectedly. Apparently it seemed that this was a small group of Sahaabah 薹 advancing towards the kuffar, but Allah 薹 sent the Malaaikah (angels) to assist the Muslims.

The great leaders of the Quraish were slain. The remainder of the Quraish began to flee the battlefield and the Muslims gave chase. Seventy of the disbelievers were killed and seventy were taken captive. Fourteen Sahaabah were martyred of whom six were from the Muhaajireen and eight from the Ansaar.

Treatment towards the captives

When the captives from Badr were brought to Madinah, Nabi ﷺ paired them and placed them in the care of the Sahaabah 👐. He commanded the Sahaabah 👐 to keep them comfortable. They fed the captives with food whilst they themselves sufficed on dates. It was decided that these captives would be ransomed. They were set free after a payment of four thousand dirhams for each captive.

Fairness and equality in Islaam

Hadhrat Abbaas 👐, the uncle of Nabi ﷺ was among the captives of Badr. At night Nabi ﷺ heard his uncle Hadhrat Abbaas 👐 groaning due to his captivity. Rasulullah ﷺ mentioned: "How will I ever be able to sleep when I can hear the groaning of my uncle?"

Subsequently the Sahaabah 👐 decided to loosen the chains tied around the hands of Hadhrat Abbaas 👐 and the other captives. As the other captives were ransomed, Abbaas 👐 was also ransomed for his freedom. He was made to pay more than the amount that the other captives paid. Four thousand dirhams were taken for the release of the average captive and those who were wealthy had to pay more. Since Hadhrat Abbaas 👐 was wealthy, he paid more than the normal ransom. The Ansaar suggested that the ransom of Hadhrat Abbaas 👐 be waived. Rasulullah ﷺ did not accept this suggestion as it was against fairness.

Similarly, Nabi ﷺ son-in-law, Abul 'Aas, was among the captives. He did not have any wealth to pay for his ransom. He sent a message to his wife, Hadhrat Zaynub رضي الله عنها who was still in Makkah to send the ransom money. She had a necklace that her mother, Hadhrat Khadijah رضي الله عنها had given her and sent it in lieu of the ransom. When Nabi ﷺ saw the necklace, tears filled his eyes and he told the Sahaabah: "If you agree then this necklace of Zaynub رضي الله عنها, which is a memory of her mother, should be returned to her." The Sahaabah 👐 willingly returned the necklace. Abul `Aas was then instructed to send Zaynub رضي الله عنها to Madinah.

Abul 'Aas ☙ accepts Islaam

Abul 'Aas ☙ was set free and came to Makkah. He fulfilled his promise and sent Hadhrat Zaynub رضي الله عنها to Madinah. Abul 'Aas ☙ was a tradesman and used to travel to Shaam (Syria) for trade. Once, on his way to Shaam, he was captured by the Muslims but was thereafter set free. Upon entering Makkah he returned the people's goods and accepted Islaam in their presence. He then addressed them saying:

"The reason I came to Makkah and accepted Islaam is to ensure that people will not say that I accepted Islaam in order to avoid paying what I had owed to the people."

Good treatment towards the captives

The captives from Badr did not have sufficient clothing. Rasulullah ﷺ provided clothing to all the captives. Hadhrat Abbaas ☙ was so tall, that there was no garment that fitted him. Abdullah bin Ubayy bin Salool (the leader of the munafiqeen) gave him his kurta. When Abdullah bin Ubayy died, Nabi ﷺ gave his own kurta to be used as a kafan in exchange for his favour to Hadhrat Abbaas ☙.

The importance of education

The captives from Badr who were unable to pay the ransom, were each asked to teach ten children in exchange for their ransom.

Hadhrat Zaid bin Thaabit ☙ learnt to read and write in this manner. From this incident we understand the importance given to education. The Muslims did not feel disgraced to study under non-Muslim tutors who were prisoners.

Other events during the year 2 A.H.

1. Nabi's ﷺ daughter Hadhrat Ruqayya رضي الله عنها passed away. The news of the victory of Badr reached Madinah when the Sahaabah ﷺ had just finished burying her.
2. Eid Salaah was performed for the first time.
3. The command of *saum* (fasting) in Ramadhan and zakah was given in this year.
4. Sadaqa-tul-Fitr, the Salaah of Eid-ul-Adha and Qurbaani were all made waajib in this year.
5. In Zul-Hijjah Hadhrat Faatima رضي الله عنها was married.

The year 3 A.H.

The Battle of Uhud

Uhud is a mountain close to Madinah. It was here on the 7th Shawwaal 3 A.H. that this battle took place. The *qabar* (grave) of Hadhrat Haroon السلام عليه is also situated here. After the defeat at Badr, the disbelievers were extremely disgraced. After returning to Makkah, they earnestly began planning their revenge. After one year, they prepared an army of three thousand youth with all the necessary equipment and set out to Madinah. They had seven hundred pieces of armour, two hundred horses and three thousand camels. They also took fourteen women to encourage the men not to flee from the battlefield.

Nabi's ﷺ uncle, Hadhrat Abbaas ؓ had accepted Islaam but remained in Makkah. He informed Nabi ﷺ of the intentions of the Quraish. Nabi ﷺ sent two Sahaabah ؓ to investigate the matter. They returned and informed Nabi ﷺ that the Quraish were outside Madinah. Rasulullah ﷺ appointed some Sahaabah to stand guard around Madinah as he feared an attack from them.

After consulting with the Sahaabah, Nabi ﷺ left Madinah with an army of one thousand soldiers. Abdullah bin Ubayy and three hundred of his followers were part of the Muslim army. On the way they deserted the Muslims and returned to Madinah. The Muslim army was now left with only seven hundred soldiers.

Children's enthusiasm for jihaad

When the Muslims came out of Madinah an inspection was conducted of the army. The youngsters who were under age were sent back. The youngsters enthusiasm for jihaad was so great that when Hadhrat Rafi` bin Khadeej ؓ was asked to return because of his young age, he stood on the tips of his toes to appear taller. He was then accepted in the army.

When Samurah bin Jundub ⚬, who was of the same age saw this, he objected: "I am able to overpower Rafi' in wrestling. If he is allowed to go in jihad, then I should also be allowed." He was then made to wrestle with Rafi' and true to his word, he dropped Rafi' ⚬. He was also allowed to join the army.

Will those who say that Islaam spread by force not feel ashamed over their lies after seeing these sacrifices? Nabi 🕮 arranged the rows of the army. Nabi 🕮 then appointed fifty archers to guard the mountain pass at the rear. There was a fear of an attack from this pass. Nabi 🕮 instructed them not to move from their position under any circumstances.

The battle began and for some time severe combat ensued. The Muslims gained the upper hand and the Quraish fled from the battlefield. The Muslims began collecting the booty. On seeing this, the archers who were posted by Rasulullah 🕮 to guard the rear, left their postions to join the others in collecting the booty. Their Ameer, Hadhrat Abdullah bin Jubair ⚬ tried to stop them from leaving their positions but they felt that there was no need to remain there anymore. Only a few Sahaabah ⚬ remained with him.

Khaalid bin Waleed ⚬, who was not yet a Muslim, was fighting against the Muslims. He saw that this area was unguarded and attacked from the rear. Hadhrat Abdullah bin Jubair ⚬ and his few companions fought very bravely but were eventually martyred. Both the armies engaged in such close combat that it was not clear who the Muslims were striking with their swords. Muslims unknowingly killed their fellow Muslim brothers. Hadhrat Mus'ab bin U'mair ⚬ was also martyred in this battle.

Dreadful news

When Hadhrat Mus'ab bin U'mair ؓ was martyred, the news spread that Nabi ﷺ was martyred. This was because Hadhrat Mus`ab ؓ resembled Nabi ﷺ. It appears in some narrations that either shaytaan or one of the disbelievers screamed that Muhammad ﷺ was killed!

When this news spread, the Muslims, began losing hope. Many great Sahaabah ؓ were in despair, but continued fighting bravely. All of them were eagerly trying to find Nabi ﷺ. The first to spot Nabi ﷺ was Hadhrat Ka'b bin Malik ؓ. He screamed aloud: "O Muslims, congratulations! Our Prophet ﷺ is safe."

On hearing this, the Muslim's spirits were lifted and the signs of despondency soon faded away. They all moved towards Rasulullah ﷺ with great joy.

In the meanwhile, the disbelievers regrouped and launched an attack towards Nabi ﷺ, but Nabi ﷺ was safe. Once, when they had surrounded Nabi ﷺ, he asked: "Who is prepared to sacrifice his life for me?" Hadhrat Ziyaad ibn Sakan ؓ and four other Sahaabah ؓ came forward and fought bravely against the disbelievers. They were all martyred. When Hadhrat Ziyaad ؓ was wounded and fell to the ground, Rasulullah ﷺ asked for him to be brought close. The Sahaabah ؓ carried him to Rasulullah ﷺ and placed his head at the mubaarak feet of Rasulullah ﷺ until he breathed his last. Subhanallah, what an honour!

Nabi's ﷺ Mubaarak face is wounded

A famous warrior from the Quraish, Abdullah bin Qami-ah passed the rows of soldiers and reached Nabi ﷺ. He struck a blow with his sword on the mubaarak face of Nabi ﷺ. This caused two links of his helmet to sink into his mubaarak face and one tooth to break.

When Hadhrat Abu Bakr ؓ came forward to remove the links, Abu U`baidah bin Jarrah ؓ took a *qasam* (oath) that he be permitted to remove it. He went forward and instead of removing them with his hands, he attempted to pull them out with his teeth. With his first attempt one link came off. He pulled it with so much force that his own tooth fell off in the process. On seeing this, Hadhrat Abu Bakr ؓ went forward to remove the second link. Again Abu U`baidah ؓ promised that he will remove the second link as well. When he pulled out the second link his second tooth also fell off. At this instance, Nabi ﷺ had fallen into a pit which the kufaar had dug to entrap the Muslims.

Bravery and sacrifice of the Sahaabah ؓ

The disbelievers attacked with much force and hoped to kill Nabi ﷺ. On seeing what was happening to Nabi ﷺ, the Sahaabah ؓ rushed to protect him. A volley of arrows and the strikes of the swords fell on the Sahaabah ؓ.

Hadhrat Abu Dujaanah ؓ bent over and acted as a shield for Nabi ﷺ. The arrows that were raining in the direction of Rasulullah ﷺ were taken on his back.

Hadhrat Talha ؓ stopped the arrows and the strikes of the swords with his body and hands, as a result of which his hand was crippled. When his body was examined after the battle, there were more than seventy wounds on his body.

One Sahaabi asked Nabi ﷺ: "What will happen to me if I am killed?" Nabi ﷺ replied: "You will enter Jannah." This Sahaabi had a few dates in his hands which he was eating. On hearing this, he threw them away and advanced into the thick of battle where he fought bravely till he was martyred.

The ruthless Quraish continued to strike at Rasulullah ﷺ, but he continued making dua for them:

$$ اَللّٰهُمَّ اغْفِرْ لِقَوْمِىْ فَاِنَّهُمْ لاَ يَعْلَمُوْن $$

O Allah! Forgive my people for verily they do not know.

Blood gushed from his Mubaarak face. Nabi ﷺ kept on wiping it with a piece of cloth. Thereafter he said that if one drop of this blood had to fall onto the ground, Allah's ﷻ (punishment) would afflict them.

In this battle twenty-two or twenty-three disbelievers were killed and seventy Muslims martyred.

The following events also occurred during this year:

1. Nabi ﷺ married Hadhrat Hafsah رضي الله عنها and Hadhrat Zaynub رضي الله عنها.
2. Intoxicants was made haraam.
3. Hadhrat Hasan ؓ was born.

The Battle of Ghatafaan

In Rabi-ul-Awwal 3 A.H. Du'thoor bin Haarith Muhaaribi marched with an army of four hundred and fifty soldiers to attack Madinah. He intended destroying the Muslims.

Nabi 🌣 and the Sahaabah 🌣 came out of Madinah to confront Du'thoor but Du'thoor and his army fled out of fear for the Muslims and hid in the mountain tops. Nabi 🌣 was then at ease and returned from the battlefield.

On their return it rained and their clothes were wet. Nabi 🌣 removed his upper garment and hung it on a tree to dry whilst he rested under its shade. The rest of the Sahaabah 🌣 were some distance away from Nabi 🌣.

Du'thoor recognized this as a good opportunity to attack Nabi 🌣 because he was alone. He approached Nabi 🌣, unsheathed his sword and asked: "Who will save you from me now?" Nabi 🌣 replied: "My Allah will save me." Du'thoor heard this and began trembling. This caused the sword to fall from his hands. Nabi 🌣 lifted the sword and asked Du'thoor: "Who will now save you from me?" "Nobody is there to save me," he replied.

Nabi 🌣 felt sorry for him and spared him. Du'thoor departed and was so affected by the noble character of Rasulullah 🌣 that not only did he accept Islaam, but after returning to his people, he began propagating Islaam amongst them with great enthusiasm.

This was the noble character of our Nabi 🌣 that caused the greatest of enemies to relent. They became deeply affected by the noble character of Rasulullah 🌣 and were honoured with the acceptance of Islaam. If any person would care to observe this objectively without any bias, can he claim that Islaam spread by the sword?

The year 4 A.H.

Bir-e-Ma'oonah

Abu Bara A'amir through deception and pretence misled Nabi ﷺ into believing that it would be beneficial if a group of Sahaabah ؓ were sent to Najd to preach Islaam. He told Nabi ﷺ that the governor of Najd was his nephew and there was no fear or danger. Secretly he planned with other tribes to kill this group. Nabi ﷺ sent a group of Sahaabah ؓ to Najd in the month of Safar 4 A.H.

This group of Sahaabah ؓ consisted of many Ulama and Qurraa. When they arrived, the tribes of A'amir, Ri'l, Zakwaan and U'sayya confronted them and this led to a battle. With the exception of Hadhrat Ka'b bin Zaid ؓ all the other Sahaabah ؓ were martyred. Nabi ﷺ was greatly grieved by this incident and for the next few days cursed these kuffaar in the fajr salaah.

During that year in the month of Shawwaal, the following events took place:

1. The birth of Hadhrat Husain ؓ
2. Nabi ﷺ married Hadhrat Umme Salimah رضي الله عنها.
3. Nabi ﷺ instructed Hadhrat Zaid bin Thabit ؓ to learn the Jewish language (Hebrew).

The year 5 A.H.

Battle of Khandaq (trench) or Battle of Ahzaab (groups)

The meaning of "ahzaab" is "groups". Various large groups from the different Arab tribes participated in this battle to destroy Madinah. It is called the Battle of Ahzaab for this reason. This war is also called the Battle of Khandaq (trench) because the Muslims dug trenches around Madinah.

The Quraish and the Jews

After Rasulullah 🖤 came to Madinah, he built good relationships with all residents of the city irrespective of their religion. Nabi 🖤 made an agreement with the Jews that they would remain united. Nabi 🖤 adhered to this agreement but the Jews were unable to tolerate Islaam's progress and secretly continued plotting against the Muslims.

When the Muslims were victorious in the Battle of Badr, they could not contain their anger and broke their agreement. In 2 A.H. the Jews from the tribe of Banu Qaynuqaa declared war against the Muslims. The Banu Nadheer also went against the Muslims. On seeing this, Nabi 🖤 began preparing for war. The Jews enclosed themselves in their forts. They were besieged for some time and thereafter banished. The Banu Qaynuqaa were banished to Shaam (Syria) and the Banu Nadheer to Khaibar.

The Quraish of Makkah, the Jews of Madinah Munawwarah and the munafiqeen, plotted as a united force against the Muslims. Hatred for the Muslims continued growing in all the tribes from Makkah to Madinah. The Battle of Zaat-ur-Riqaa' that had taken place on the 10th Muharram 5 A.H. and the Battle of Dowma-tul-Jundul which had taken place in Rabi-ul-Awwal 5 A.H. were the outcomes of this plot. The Battle of Banu-ul-Mustaliq that took place on the 2nd Shabaan 5 A.H. was also as a result of this plot.

For some time, the Quraish continued planning against the Muslims. Eventually, their plans became a reality, in Zil-Qa'dah 5 A.H. All these groups gathered their forces and decided to attack Madinah. An army of ten thousand fierce warriors, which later doubled, marched towards Madinah to attack the Muslims.

When this information reached Nabi ﷺ, he gathered the Sahaabah ﷺ and consulted them. Hadhrat Salmaan Farsi ﷺ suggested that it was inappropriate to go out of Madinah to fight. Instead, trenches should be dug on the side where there was fear of the disbelievers attacking. This was due to the danger presented by the Banu Quraizah who were still in Madinah, as well as the munaafiqeen (hypocrites) who were present amongst the people of Madinah.

Thus, Nabi ﷺ together with three thousand Sahaabah ﷺ prepared to dig these trenches. Whilst the Sahaabah ﷺ were digging, they encountered a large boulder which they were unable to break. Nabi ﷺ miraculously broke the boulder with just one blow. Nabi ﷺ and the Sahaabah ﷺ toiled tirelessly day and night to dig the trench.

The disbelievers placed Madinah under siege for almost fifteen days. The Banu Quraizah, whom the Muslims feared, sided with the disbelievers and this increased their number.

The siege caused great uneasiness among the Muslims. The food provisions were exhausted and due to insufficient rations, people were suffering from starvation. In addition, there was no way of going out of Madinah.

Eventually, the Sahaabah ﷺ who were in a state of distress approached Nabi ﷺ complaining of hunger. They lifted their garments showing Nabi ﷺ that they each had a stone tied to their stomachs. Rasulullah ﷺ lifted his garment and showed the Sahaabah ﷺ two stones tied to his mubaarak stomach.

When the disbelievers realised that they were unable to cross the trench, they began throwing stones and shooting arrows at the Muslims. The Muslims also counter attacked. This encounter continued for a long time which caused Nabi ﷺ to miss four of his Salaah.

The unseen assistance of Allah ﷻ

Allah ﷻ assisted the Muslim army in this trying moment and sent a strong wind that uprooted the tents of the disbelievers from the ground and overturned their pots that were over blazing fires. This left the disbelievers devastated and without any provisions. Furthermore, Nu'aim bin Mas'ood ؓ had carried out a strategic plan that caused confusion and disunity amongst the ranks of the kuffar army. Thus, the kuffar were totally uprooted and fled the battlefield.

Various other events during the year 5 A.H.

1. Haj was made fardh (compulsory) in this year. (Although there are other views.)
2. In Jumad-ul-Ula, Nabi's ﷺ grandson Abdullah bin Uthmaan ؓ passed away. He was Hadhrat Ruqayya's رضي الله عنها son.
3. Towards the end of Shawwaal, Hadhrat Aaishah's رضي الله عنها mother passed away
4. In Zil-Qa'dah, Nabi ﷺ married Hadhrat Zaynub bint Jahsh ؓ.
5. There was a tremor in Madinah.
6. There was a lunar eclipse (the moon came between the sun and the earth).

We have read that the tribe of Banu Quraizah joined the disbelievers in the Battle of Ahzaab and broke their agreement with Rasulullah ﷺ. After the battle of Ahzaab, Nabi ﷺ attacked them. They sought refuge in their fort for twenty-five days. Eventually, they became helpless and requested Nabi ﷺ to appoint the leader of the Ows Hadhrat Sa'd bin Mu`aaz ؓ to decide their fate and they would accept whatever decision he made. Hadhrat Sa'd bin Mu'aaz 鍈 passed the decision in accordance to the Jewish law:

(a)   Those men who can fight must be killed
(b)   Their women and children must be taken as slaves
(c)   Their wealth should be distributed amongst the Muslims

Three other battles, besides the Battle of Khandaq and the battle against the Banu Quraizah, were also fought during this year. They were:

1. Zat-ur-Riqaa'
2. Dowma-tul-Jundul
3. Banul-Mustaliq

However, fighting only took place in the battle of Banul-Mustaliq and Allah 鍈 granted the Muslims victory.

The year 6 A.H.

Treaty of Hudaybiyyah, Bay'at-ur-Ridhwan and the invitation of Islaam to the kings

Hudaybiyyah is a place about one manzil (25.5 km.) from Makkah. There is a well in this place named Hudaybiyyah after which this place is named. The treaty of Hudaybiyyah was made here.

This event occurred at the beginning of Zil-Qa'dah 6 A.H., when Nabi ﷺ tied the ihram for 'Umrah and set out towards Makkah. A large group of Sahaabah ﷺ, approximately 1400 to 1500, joined Rasulullah ﷺ from Madinah. They marched towards Makkah and camped at Hudaybiyyah.

Nabi's ﷺ mu'jizah (miracle)

The well at Hudaybiyyah had dried up. Through the miracle of Nabi ﷺ, the well once again became full and all the Sahaabah ﷺ quenched their thirst.

When the disbelievers learnt of the intentions of Nabi ﷺ, they decided to stop him from entering Makkah. Nabi ﷺ sent Hadhrat Uthmaan ﷺ to Makkah to inform the disbelievers that they had come only to perform U'mrah. When Hadhrat Uthmaan ﷺ reached Makkah, the disbelievers detained him.

A rumour spread that the disbelievers had killed Hadhrat Uthmaan ﷺ. When the news reached Nabi ﷺ, he gathered the Sahaabah ﷺ under an acacia tree and instructed them to take bay'at (pledge allegiance) upon jihaad. This is mentioned in the Qur'aan as Bay'at-ur-Ridhwaan. Later they learnt that Hadhrat Uthmaan ﷺ was not killed by the Makkans and that this was only a rumour.

The Muslims and disbelievers agreed to sign a treaty so that both sides would have the opportunity of being at peace. The Quraish sent Suhail bin A`mr to settle the conditions of the agreement which would be applicable for ten years. The following was agreed upon:

1. The Muslims should return to Madinah immediately.
2. The Muslims would be allowed to come to Makkah the following year, but only for three days.
3. They should not come with their weapons. If swords are brought, they should be kept in their sheaths (cover for swords).
4. Any Muslim still in Makkah will not be allowed to return with the Muslims to Madinah. No Muslim should be prevented from remaining in Makkah if he wished to do so. If any Muslim from Makkah came to Madinah he would have to be sent back. On the contrary if any Muslim from Madinah came to Makkah he would not be sent back to Madinah.

The Sahaabah 🜪 were not pleased with this treaty. Hadhrat Umar 🜪 expressed this to Nabi 醬. Nabi 醬 replied that I have been commanded by Allah 🜪 to do so. Allah 🜪 revealed *Surah Fatah*, wherein this treaty was termed as an open victory. Hence, subsequent events confirmed the fact that this treaty was a clear victory for the Muslims. The Muslims gained many advantages through this treaty. Some of these include:

(a) Previously, due to the wars with the Quraish and other tribes, the Muslims were unable to access other tribes and regions to preach Islaam. Now the doors were open for them.
(b) The Muslims were now able to meet and interact with the disbelievers as a result of which the disbelievers would have an opportunity to witness Islaam. Thereafter, they began entering into the fold of Islaam. In a short period the number of Muslims increased.
(c) The disbelievers were always trying to dishonour and humiliate the Muslims. They tried to wipe out their existence but were never successful in this. Eventually they were forced to sign a treaty with the Muslims, whom they always considered to be weak. It is

evident that for an apparently strong party to reduce themselves to negotiate with a weaker party is a victory for the weaker party who in this case were the Muslims. Thus it becomes clear why the Qur'aan refers to this incident as *"Fath-e-Mubeen"* which means "A clear victory."

There were two battles fought during this year:

1. Battle of Lihyaan
2. Battle of Ghaabah also known as Zi Qarad.

Eleven sarayaa were also sent in this year. Hadhrat Khaalid bin Waleed ﷺ and Amr bin A'as ﷺ also accepted Islaam in this year.

After the treaty of Hudaybiyyah, the Muslims received the opportunity to spread Islaam and the enemies witnessed its beauty first hand.

Invitation of Islaam to the kings of the world

Nabi ﷺ wished that the message of Islaam should reach the kings of the world. The following are the names of the kings to whom letters were sent, their responses and the names of the Sahaabah ﷺ who took the letters:

1. A'mr bin Umayya ﷺ was sent to As-hamah, Najashi, the king of Habsha (Ethiopia). On receiving the letter of Nabi ﷺ, he placed the letter on his eyes. He descended from his throne, sat on the ground and accepted Islaam wholeheartedly.

2. Dihya Kalbi ﷺ was sent to Hiraql, the emperor of Rome. He was aware from previous scriptures, that Nabi ﷺ was a true nabi. He wished to accept Islaam, but this angered his subjects. He feared that if he became a Muslim, his people would take away his leadership and this prevented him from accepting Islaam.

3. Abdullah bin Hudhaafah ﷺ was sent to the proud Kisrah, Khosro Parwez, the leader of Persia. This wretched person disgraced the

mubaarak letter of Nabi ﷺ and tore the letter to pieces. When this news reached Nabi ﷺ, he cursed him saying: "May Allah ﷻ tear his kingdom as he tore my letter into pieces." How could the dua of Nabi ﷺ go unanswered? After a short period of time, Khosro Parwez was killed by his very own son Sherooyah in a merciless way.

4. Haatib bin Abi Balta`a ؓ was sent to the leader of Egypt and Alexandria (Maqowqas). Allah ﷻ inspired him with the truth of Islaam and love for Nabi ﷺ in his heart. He treated Hadhrat Haatib ؓ very kindly and sent gifts for Nabi ﷺ among which were Maariya Qibtiyyah رضي الله عنها and a white mule, whose name was Duldul. It is mentioned in one narration that he also gifted one thousand dinaars and twenty sets of clothing to Nabi ﷺ.

5. A'mr bin A'as ؓ was sent to the leaders of Omaan. Their names were Ja'far and Abdullah. They were convinced with the truthfulness of Nabi ﷺ through their research of the previous scriptures and both of them accepted Islaam. They immediately began collecting zakaat from their subjects and handed it over to Hadhrat A'mr bin A'as ؓ.

Khaalid bin Waleed ؓ and A'mr bin A'as ؓ accept Islaam

Until that time Hadhrat Khaalid bin Waleed ؓ fought in every battle against the Muslims. It was through his efforts that the disbelievers held firm in most battles especially in Uhud. However, after the treaty of Hudaybiyyah he travelled from Makkah to Madinah on his own and became a Muslim. On the way he met Hadhrat A'mr bin A'as ؓ who was travelling for the same reason. Both of them reached Madinah together and accepted Islaam at the same time.

The year 7 A.H.

Battle of Khaibar

When the Banu Nadheer were banished from Madinah, they settled in Khaibar. They began inciting the neighbouring tribes to fight against the Muslims. There was a need to take control over their base and to destroy their power. That is why in Muharram or Jumadul-Ula 7 A.H., Nabi ﷺ and six hundred Sahaabah ؓ left for Khaibar. Four hundred Sahaabah ؓ were on foot and two hundred were mounted.

Allah ﷻ granted the Muslims victory after a battle and they gained control over all the forts of the Jews.

Hadhrat Ali ؓ played a significant role in this jihaad and lifted the door of Khaibar himself whereas seventy men were unable to even shake it. For this reason, he was known as the conqueror of Khaibar. It appears in some narrations that Nabi ﷺ used this door as a shield. The following conditions were laid down in the treaty with the Banu Nadheer:

1. They will remain in Khaibar as long as the Muslims permitted and when the Muslims wished to remove them they would have to move.
2. A portion of their crops should be handed over to the Muslims.

Conquest of Fadak

In this journey Nabi ﷺ travelled to Fadak. Before they could engage in battle, a treaty was signed with the Muslims. There were no other wars besides these in the year 5 A.H. During that year Nabi ﷺ sent various delegations to different places.

U'mra-tul-Qadha

Nabi ﷺ performed the U'mrah, which was missed the previous year when the treaty of Hudaybiyyah was signed. It was stated therein that the Muslims would only be allowed to perform U'mrah in the coming year and would be allowed to stay in Makkah for only three days.

Nabi ﷺ and the Sahaabah ؓ adhered to this treaty and prepared for Umrah after a full year had passed. After performing U'mrah they returned to Madinah. During this journey Nabi ﷺ married Hadhrat Maymoonah رضي الله عنها.

The year 8 A.H.

Sariyyah to Muta

Muta is the name of a place in Shaam (Syria) approximately two manzils (51.5km.) from Baitul Maqdis and close to the city of Balqaan. The cause of this war was that Nabi 🌸 sent Hadhrat Harith bin U`mair 🌸 with the invitation of Islaam to Sharjeel, the ruler of Basrah. Unfortunately, Sharjeel reacted with aggression and killed Hadhrat Harith bin U'mair 🌸.

In 8 A.H., Nabi 🌸 sent an army of three thousand Sahaabah 🌸 to confront Sharjeel, who prepared an army of nearly one hundred and fifty thousand soldiers. The battle took place in Muta.

Allah 🌸 placed such awe for this small group of Muslims in the hearts of the Romans that they fled from the battlefield and the Muslims gained victory.

Three leaders of the Muslim army were made shaheed in this battle:

- Hadhrat Zaid bin Haritha 🌸
- Hadhrat Ja'far 🌸
- Hadhrat Abdullah bin Rawaaha 🌸.

After these three Sahaabah 🌸 were made shaheed, Hadhrat Khaalid bin Waleed 🌸 took charge of the Muslim army and thereafter the Muslims gained victory. From then, Hadhrat Khaalid 🌸 was given the title of Saifullah (The Sword of Allah 🌸).

Conquest of Makkah

At the time of the Treaty of Hudaybiyyah the Banu Bakr joined the Quraish and the Banu Khuza'ah joined the Muslims. Before two years passed, the Banu Bakr attacked the Banu Khuza`ah killing their women and children. The Quraish assisted the Banu Bakr in this fight. When the Banu Khuza`ah asked the Banu Bakr for safety in the name of Allah, they replied that they have no regard for Allah 鐵"

Those who remained from the Banu Khuza'ah came to Madinah seeking the help of the Muslims. A'mar bin Saalim recited a heart-rending poem to Nabi 鐵 wherein he sought his help. On hearing this poem Nabi 鐵 became restless and sent a messenger to the Quraish requesting them to re-affirm the treaty. Nabi 鐵 informed them that if they did not accept the conditions that were laid down, the treaty of Hudaybiyyah would be cancelled. The Quraish were not pleased with the conditions and chose to cancel the treaty.

Eventually, Rasulullah 鐵 began preparing for jihaad. On Wednesday, 10th Ramadhan 8 A.H. after Asr, Nabi 鐵 with an army of ten thousand strong left Madinah. On reaching Makkah, Hadhrat Khaalid bin Waleed 鐵 was instructed to enter Makkah with a group of Sahaabah from the upper end. Nabi 鐵 instructed him not to confront those who did not attack them.

From the other end, Nabi 鐵 entered Makkah on his camel with Hadhrat Usama 鐵. Nabi 鐵 wore a black turban and was reciting the aayaat (verses) of Surah Fath. With total humility and modesty Nabi 鐵 announced:

"Whoever enters the Musjid-e-Haraam will be safe, whoever stays indoors will be safe, the wounded will not be killed, the captives will not be killed and those who try to escape will not be chased."

On Friday, 20th Ramadhan, Nabi 鐵 made tawaaf of the Ka`bah. There were three hundred and sixty idols around the Ka`bah. When Nabi 鐵

passed each idol, he pointed towards it with his stick and it would fall to the ground on its face. At this juncture Rasulullah ﷺ was reciting the verse:

$$جَآءَ الْحَقُّ وَ زَهَقَ الْبَاطِلُ اِنَّ الْبَاطِلَ كَانَ زَهُوْقًا$$

The truth has come and falsehood has perished. Most definitely falsehood is bound to perish.

Treatment of the disbelievers after the conquest of Makkah

After completing the tawaaf of the Ka'bah, Nabi ﷺ called for Uthmaan bin Talha Shaybi ﷺ and asked him to open the Ka'bah. Nabi ﷺ went into the Ka'bah Shareef and then to the Maqaam-e-Ibraheem and performed Salaah behind it.

On that day Nabi ﷺ confronted those who had planned to kill him. They had banished him from his hometown, afflicted his Sahaabah ﷺ with much difficulties, distress, suffering and engaged the Muslims in numerous battles.

All were waiting fearfully, expecting revenge to be taken against them. However, Nabi ﷺ who was *Rahmate Aalam* (a mercy unto mankind) addressed them saying:

$$أَنْتُمُ الْطُّلَقَاءُ لَا تَثْرِيْبَ عَلَيْكُمُ الْيَوْمَ$$

You all are free. There is no blame on you today.

This was the sublime character of that gracious personality who was a mercy unto mankind!

Is it still possible for those who are prejudiced to say that Islaam spread by the sword?

The noble character of Nabi ﷺ and Abu Sufyaan's acceptance of Islaam

Abu Sufyaan, the flag bearer of the Quraish and the commander in most of the battles against the Muslims, came out of Makkah to gain information of the Muslim army. The Sahaabah ؇ captured him. When he was brought in front of Nabi ﷺ, he instructed that Abu Sufyaan be set free. This had such an effect on Abu Sufyaan that he immediately accepted Islaam. This raised his status to such an extent, that he is now refered to as Hadhrat Abu Sufyaan ؇.

On the day of the conquest of Makkah, someone approached Nabi ﷺ trembling and awe stricken. Rasulullah ﷺ the embodiment of mercy comforted him with the following words: "I am not a king. I am the son of an ordinary woman." This incident emphasises the noble and humble character of Rasulullah ﷺ.

After the conquest of Makkah, Rasulullah ﷺ remained in Makkah for fifteen days. The Ansaar thought that Nabi ﷺ would probably remain in Makkah and they would be deprived of his noble and august company. When Rasulullah ﷺ heard this he said:

"No. My life and my death will be with you." Thereafter, Nabi ﷺ returned to Madinah after appointing Hadhrat A'ttaab bin Usaid ؇ as the governor of Makkah.

Battle of Hunain

After the conquest of Makkah, the Arabs began entering into Islaam in large numbers. Many of them had conviction in the truthfulness of Islaam but had not previously accepted due to fear of the Quraish. The Quraish were now defeated and this obstacle was removed. This is why many now accepted Islaam.

Those Arabs who did not accept Islaam did not have the strength to oppose the Muslims. However, there were two tribes, the Hawaazin and Thaqeef who could not tolerate the rise of Islaam. They prepared to wage war against the Muslims and set out towards Makkah.

When the news reached Rasulullah 卌, he gathered an army of twelve thousand Sahaabah 卌 to fight them. The army consisted of ten thousand Muhaajireen and Ansaar and two thousand who accepted Islaam at the conquest of Makkah.

On the 6th Shawwaal this army left Makkah. When they reached the valley of Hunain, the enemy who were prepared and waiting in ambush attacked the Muslims from all directions. The front section of the Muslim army scattered since there was no preparation for battle as yet. This seemed to be the apparent cause. However the Qur'aan mentions that the real cause for this was that some of the Muslims placed their confidence in their large numbers. The initial setback was an admonition and a rebuke from Allah Ta'ala.

Allah 卌 in order to warn them, allowed this to occur so that the Muslims would realise that victory and defeat is not based on strength and number, but only on the assistance of Allah 卌.

This is why the Muslims were victorious in Badr despite their lack of means yet suffered this setback in Hunain despite their strength and numbers.

Nabi 🪶 wore a double layer of armour and rode a white mule called Duldul. Seeing the condition of the Muslim army, Nabi 🪶 commanded Hadhrat Abbaas ⚜ to summon the Muslims. His inspiring call gave courage to the Muslims and once again the battle ensued between the disbelievers and Muslims.

A great mu'jizah (miracle)

Nabi 🪶 picked a handful of sand and threw it towards the disbelievers. Allah 🪶 caused the sand to go into their eyes. The disbelievers were overawed and fled from the battlefield. The Muslims eventually gained victory. Only four Muslims were martyred whereas more than seventy disbelievers were killed.

The Muslims took possession of all the enemy's belongings as booty amongst which were twenty four thousand camels, more than forty thousand goats and four thousand awqiya (489,888 kgs.) of silver. All this was distributed among the Muslims. The new Muslims from Makkah were given a larger share of the booty.

Battle of Taaif

After the Banu Thaqeef and Hawaazin were defeated in Hunain, they took refuge in the fort of Taaif. Nabi 🪶 followed them to Taaif. For approximately eighteen days the Muslims laid siege to the fort. During this time the people of Taaif shot many arrows at the Muslims due to which a large number of Muslims were wounded and twelve were made shaheed.

Hadhrat Salmaan Farsi ⚜ suggested that the Muslim army respond by using a catapult, which was like a canon of that time. Besides this, no real fighting took place. When Nabi 🪶 left Taaif and camped at Ji`rranah, the people of Taaif came to Nabi 🪶 and requested him to handover those who were captured at Hunain. Nabi 🪶 agreed and handed them over. After returning to Madinah, a delegation from Taaif came to Madinah and accepted Islaam.

U'mrah from Ji'irranah

Thereafter, Nabi 🌸 performed U'mrah from Ji'rranah where he tied his ihraam and left for Makkah. Nabi 🌸 returned to Madinah on the 6th Zul-Qa'dah 8 A.H.

The year 9 A.H.

The Battle of Tabuk

After returning from Taaif, Nabi 🌸 remained in Madinah until the middle of 9 A.H. He was informed that *Hiraql* (Heracles) was preparing an army in Tabuk to attack the Muslims after the disbelievers were defeated in Muta. Nabi 🌸 began preparations for jihaad even though the Muslims were in a distressed condition. This condition was brought about by hardship and shortages due to the drought prevalent at that time.

The Sahaabah ⚜ were a group who were always ready to sacrifice and thus they immediately commenced preparations. When an appeal was made for contributions towards the war, Hadhrat Abu Bakr ⚜ brought all his belongings. Hadhrat Umar ⚜ brought half his belongings and Hadhrat Uthmaan ⚜ presented 900 camels, 100 horses and ten thousand dinaars. Similarly, other Sahaabah ⚜ donated towards the jihaad according to their capability. The women donated their jewellery.

On a Thursday in Rajab, Nabi 🌸 left Madinah for Tabuk with twenty thousand Sahaabah. Muhammad bin Maslamah ⚜ was appointed the governor of Madinah for this period. The Muslim army had approximately thirty thousand pieces of weapons and ten thousand horses.

Few mu'jizaat (miracles)

Whilst travelling, Rasulullah ﷺ saw Hadhrat Abu Zar Ghifaari ؓ travelling aloof from the others. Upon seeing this, Rasulullah ﷺ commented that Abu Zar ؓ will remain aloof from the world and will pass away aloof from the world. This is exactly what happened later as is recorded in the books of history.

In this battle, Nabi's ﷺ camel went missing. Nabi ﷺ was informed through wahi (revelation) that its bridle had become entangled to a tree. Nabi ﷺ went to that tree and found the camel as had been revealed to him.

When Nabi ﷺ and the Sahaabah reached Tabuk, they found that the enemy had fled and Hiraql had escaped to Hims. Nabi ﷺ sent Hadhrat Khaalid bin Waleed ؓ to capture Ukaydir Nasraani and informed him that Ukaydir would be found hunting at night. When Hadhrat Khaalid ؓ apprehended him, he was indeed hunting and Hadhrat Khaalid ؓ captured him.

Since no battle was fought, Nabi ﷺ returned after staying in Tabuk for fifteen to twenty days. This was the last expedition of Nabi ﷺ. Nabi ﷺ returned to Madinah in Ramadhan 9 A.H. The Romans were terrified of the Muslims throughout this expedition and thus remained inactive. Thereafter Yuhanna, the governor of Aylah came to Rasulullah ﷺ and the governors of other areas also arrived. They entered into an agreement with Nabi ﷺ and promised to pay *kharaaj* (land taxes) in return for which, Nabi ﷺ granted them security.

Musjid-e-Dhiraar

The munaafiqeen constructed a building in Quba, which they called a musjid. They met here to plot against the Muslims. Nabi ﷺ was informed through *wahi* (revelation) that the building was not a Musjid. After returning from Tabuk, Nabi ﷺ ordered the building to be demolished.

Arrival of delegations

The Muslims got the opportunity to spread Islaam on a large scale once the roads became safe after the Treaty of Hudaybiyya had been signed. That is why the Qur'aan refers to this treaty as a *fath-e-mubeen* (clear victory). There were, however, still a few people who were prevented from accepting Islaam due to pressure from the Quraish.

The Conquest of Makkah removed this obstacle and the message of the Qur'aan reached every home. The Qur'aan, with its unique miraculous qualities, left a firm impression on the hearts of everyone. Those who could not tolerate the Muslims or Islaam, were now eagerly coming from distant places to Nabi 🌸 to accept Islaam. Willingly and happily, they accepted Islaam and were now prepared to even sacrifice their lives for Islaam. Most of these delegations came in 9 A.H. The number of Muslims increased to such an extent that when Nabi 🌸 performed Haj in 10 A.H. more than one hundred thousand Muslims joined him. The number of those who were unable to perform Haj, was more than one hundred thousand.

Hadhrat Abu Bakr 🌸, the Ameer of Haj

After returning from Tabuk in 9 A.H., Nabi 🌸 appointed Hadhrat Abu Bakr 🌸 as the *ameer* (leader) of Haj and sent him to Makkah.

The year 10 A.H.

Haj

Haj had already been made fardh before 10 A.H. Nabi ﷺ left for haj on the 25th Zul-Qa`dah 10 A.H. with the noble Sahaabah ؓ who had joined him. They numbered over a hundred thousand. Nabi ﷺ tied his ihraam at Zul-Hulaifah, six miles from Madinah. They reached Makkah on Saturday, 4th Zil-Hijjah and thereafter performed haj.

Khutbah at 'Arafaat

On the 9th Zul-Hijjah after reaching Arafaat, Nabi ﷺ delivered a very inspiring khutbah which was full of advice and wisdom. This was the final message of the final Rasul ﷺ. The following lines of the khutbah should be inscribed on the heart of every Muslim:

O people! Listen to me so that I can explain all those things that are necessary. I do not know whether we will be able to gather next year.

The life, wealth and honour of a Muslim is sacred until the Day of Qiyaamah as is the sanctity of today (Day of Arafah), this month (Zul-Hijjah) and this city (Makkah). Each person should fulfil the trust for which he is responsible and accountable

O people! Your wives have rights over you and so too, do you have rights over them.

O people! All Muslims are brothers. The wealth of another person is not lawful without his consent. Do not become disbelievers after my death by fighting with each another. I leave with you the Book of Allah. If you hold steadfast to its laws, you will never be misguided.

O people! Your Rabb (Lord) is one and your father (Aadam عليه السلام) is one. You are all the children of Aadam عليه السلام and Aadam عليه السلام was created from sand. The most honoured amongst you is he who has the most fear of Allah ﷻ. No Arab holds virtue over a non-Arab except by virtue of his taqwa (fear of Allah). Remember! I have conveyed the message. O Allah! You are my Witness that I have conveyed the message. Those present, should convey the message to those who are absent.

After performing haj, Nabi ﷺ remained in Makkah for a few days and thereafter returned to Madinah.

The year 11 A.H.

Sariyyah of Hadhrat Usaama ؓ

After returning from Makkah Mu`azzamah, Nabi ﷺ prepared an army on Monday the 26ᵗʰ Safar 11 A.H. to fight the Romans. Amongst the soldiers were many leading Sahaabah like Hadhrat Abu Bakr Siddeeq ؓ, Hadhrat Umar Farooq ؓ and Hadhrat Abu U`baidah bin Jarrah ؓ. Nabi ﷺ appointed Usama ؓ as the ameer (leader) of this army. This was the last army that Nabi ﷺ arranged himself. This army had not yet left Madinah when Nabi ﷺ fell ill. Nabi ﷺ thereafter passed away and Hadhrat Abu Bakr ؓ dispatched this army.

The final illness of Nabi ﷺ

On Wednesday, 28ᵗʰ Safar 11 A.H. Nabi ﷺ visited Baqee`-ul-Gharqad (graveyard in Madinah) where he made dua for the inmates of the graves. After returning from the graveyard, Nabi ﷺ experienced a headache and thereafter developed a fever, which lasted for thirteen days. In this condition Nabi ﷺ left this world.

During this sickness, according to his routine, Nabi ﷺ stayed each night at a different wife's house. When Nabi ﷺ fell extremely ill, he sought permission from the other azwaaj-e-mutahharaat (noble wives) to stay at Hadhrat Aa'ishah's رضي الله عنها home. All the azwaaj-e-mutahharaat granted him permission.

Hadhrat Abu Bakr ؓ leads the salaah

Nabi's ﷺ illness gradually worsened to such an extent that he was unable to go to the Musjid. Rasulullah ﷺ then instructed Hadhrat Abu Bakr ؓ to lead the Salaah. Hadhrat Abu Bakr ؓ led approximately seventeen salaah during the illness of Sayyidinah Rasulullah ﷺ.

On one occasion, Hadhrat Abu Bakr ؓ and Hadhrat Abbaas ؓ passed a group of Ansaar who were grieving. When they were asked the reason for their crying they replied that they were crying in remembrance of the majlis (gathering) of Rasulullah ﷺ.

Hadhrat Abbaas ؓ related this to Nabi ﷺ. Hearing this, Nabi ﷺ came out of his home leaning on the shoulders of Hadhrat Ali ؓ and Hadhrat Fadhl bin Abbaas ؓ whilst Hadhrat Abbaas ؓ walked ahead of them. Nabi ﷺ ascended the mimbar but was unable to climb to the top. He sat on the first step and delivered a remarkable speech to the grieving people. Part of it is as follows:

O people! I know that you fear your nabi passing away. Did any of the Ambiyaa who came in the past remain alive forever? I will be meeting my Creator and you will also be meeting me. Our meeting place will be at the Howdh-e-Kowthar (pond of Kowthar).

Whoever desires to drink from this pond on the Day of Qiyaamah should prevent his hands and tongue from engaging in useless pursuits and things that do not concern him.

My parting advice to you is to treat the Muhaajireen kindly and I instruct the Muhaajireen to remain united and show kindness to one another.

Further, Rasulullah ﷺ advised that as long as people obey Allah ﷻ and follow His commands, their rulers will be just and will treat them accordingly and if they disobey Allah ﷻ, their rulers will deal with them unjustly and treat them without mercy.

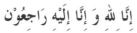

Thereafter, Nabi ﷺ went to his room and emerged only three or five days before his demise. His mubaarak head was bound with a cloth. At that time, Hadhrat Abu Bakr ؓ was leading the Salaah. On seeing Nabi ﷺ he began moving back. Nabi ﷺ signalled him not to move and sat on his left hand side. After the Salaah, Nabi ﷺ delivered a short khutbah wherein he mentioned:

Abu Bakr ؓ has been most kind to me. If I had to take anyone as a *khaleel* (bosom friend) after Allah ﷻ, I would have taken Abu Bakr ؓ as a *khaleel*. But there can be no *khaleel* (bosom friend) besides Allah ﷻ. Therefore, Abu Bakr ؓ is my brother and a companion. With the exception of Abu Bakr ؓ, everyone should block his door that leads into the Musjid.

Muhaddith Ibne Hibbaan رحمة الله عليه after narrating this Hadith, states that this Hadith is a clear indication that Hadhrat Abu Bakr ؓ was to be the Khalifah after Rasulullah ﷺ.

Thereafter, on Monday the 12ᵗʰ Rabi-ul-Awwal, whilst the Sahaabah ؓ were performing the Fajr Salaah behind Hadhrat Abu Bakr ؓ, Nabi ﷺ raised the curtain in his room, looked at the Sahaabah ؓ and smiled. On seeing Nabi ﷺ, Hadhrat Abu Bakr ؓ began to move backwards and out of happiness the Sahaabah ؓ were unable to concentrate in their Salaah. Nabi ﷺ indicated to them to complete the Salaah and he lowered the curtain. Nabi ﷺ never emerged from his room thereafter.

On this day after the Zuhr Salaah, Nabi ﷺ left this worldly abode and went to meet his Creator, Allah ﷻ,

إِنَّا لله وَ إِنَّا إِلَيْه رَاجِعُوْن

To Allah do we belong and to Him shall we return

Nabi ﷺ was buried after two days, on Wednesday, at the time of sehri (early dawn). According to the narration of Bukhaari Shareef, Nabi ﷺ was sixty-three years old at the time of his demise.

The last words of Nabi ﷺ

Hadhrat Aa'ishah رضي الله عنها mentioned that during this illness, Nabi ﷺ would at times lift the sheet from his face and say:

The curse of Allah ﷻ befell the Christians and the Jews because they transformed the graves of their Ambiyaa into places of worship."

Nabi ﷺ desired that those who believe in him should not do the same.

Alas! How many Muslims are involved in this deed, where they have made the graves of the pious into places of worship?

Hadhrat Aa'ishah رضي الله عنها narrates that towards the end, Nabi ﷺ would raise his sight towards the sky and say:

$$\text{أَللّٰهُمَّ الرَّفِيْقَ الْأَعْلَى}$$

O Allah! (grant me the companionship) of The One who is Most Kind and Most High.

In one narration it is mentioned that the words: الصَّلٰوة الصَّلٰوة *(be mindful of Salaah, be mindful of Salaah)* were constantly repeated by Nabi ﷺ.

When the news of the demise of Nabi ﷺ reached the Sahaabah ؓ, they could not contain themselves. Hadhrat Umar ؓ was so overtaken by grief that he began aggresively denying the demise of Rasulullah ﷺ. Besides him there were many other Sahaabah who were worried and in a state of confusion.

Hadhrat Abu Bakr ؓ delivered a short khutbah and encouraged the Sahaabah to adopt sabr (patience). He also mentioned:

"Whoever used to worship Muhammad ﷺ, then let him know that Muhammad ﷺ has passed away and whoever used to worship

Allah ﷻ, then let him know that Allah ﷻ is *Hayyun Qayyoom* (Ever living) and He is alive today."

Hearing this, the Sahaabah ؓ regained their senses. They realised that the most important matter after the demise of Nabi ﷺ was the appointment of a khalifah. They feared disorder in many *Deeni* and worldly matters, especially the fulfillment of the burial rites of Sayyidinah Rasulullah ﷺ. Therefore, there was a delay in the burial of Nabi ﷺ and it was only on Wednesday night that Nabi ﷺ was finally buried. The grave of Nabi ﷺ was dug in the room of Hadhrat Aa'ishah رضي الله عنها and Nabi ﷺ was buried therein.

75

The *Mubaarak* (blessed) features of Nabi 襲

Rasulullah 襲 was not very tall nor was he short. Nabi 襲 was of a moderate height. His mubaarak head was fairly large and his beard was thick. There were a few strands of white hair on his mubaarak head and beard. Some have mentioned that there were twenty to twenty five strands of white hair.

Nabi's 襲 face was extremely handsome and bright. Whoever saw the mubaarak face of Nabi 襲 described it to be brighter than the fourteenth moon.

The perspiration of Nabi 襲 had a unique fragrance. When the perspiration dripped from his mubaarak face, it would appear as if they were pearls.

Hadhrat Anas 襲 has reported that the skin of Nabi 襲 was softer than silk and the scent that emanated from his body was more fragrant than musk and amber.

The seal of nubuwat

The seal of nubuwat was between the shoulder blades of Nabi 襲. closer to the right hand side. This seal which had a special significance, was mentioned in the previous books and by the Ambiyaa of the past. The Ulama of the Bani Israeel, on seeing the seal, would readily recognise that Rasulullah 襲 was the very same final prophet, regarding whom the Ambiyaa of the past had given glad tidings.

Nabi's 襲 hair reached his shoulders and at times it reached his earlobes. Nabi 襲 combed his hair and applied surmah to his eyes. However, Nabi 襲 eyes always appeared as if surmah had been applied to them naturally. Nabi 襲 eyes were extremely beautiful and wide, with very dark pupils and reddish streaks within.

There was a long attractive streak of hair running from his chest to his navel. When Nabi 🌸 walked, he placed his foot firmly on the ground. It seemed as if he was descending from a high place.

Clothing of Nabi 🌸

Nabi 🌸 had very simple clothing. The normal clothing of Rasulullah 🌸 consisted of a lungi (piece of cloth wrapped around the lower part of the body), kurta (upper garment), topee (hat), jubba (robe) and a shawl. There were also patches on them. Nabi's 🌸 garments were white in colour. He also had a Yemeni shawl with green and red stripes. It was famously known as *Burdun Yamaaniyyun*.

Topee - The topee of Nabi 🌸 was flat and would stick to his mubaarak head.

A'maamah (Turban) - Nabi 🌸 wore a topee under his turban. The tails of the turban hung between his shoulders. At times it would hang at the back, at times on the right and at times below the chin.

Trousers - It is established that Nabi 🌸 did buy a trouser and liked it. However, it is not established whether he actually wore one.

Kurta (upper garment) - Nabi 🌸 loved the kurta. The collar extended to near the chest. At times the buttons were left open.

Lungi (lower garment) - Nabi's 🌸 lungi reached up to his shins.

Khuf (leather socks) - Nabi 🌸 used leather khufs and made masah over it at the time of wudhu.

Pillow - Nabi's 🌸 pillow was made of leather and was stuffed with pieces of bark from the date (khajoor) palm. Nabi 🌸 mostly slept on a straw mat.

Footwear - Nabi's 襚 shoes were similar to a sandal. The bottom had a leather layer and there were two straps attached to it through which his mubaarak toes would fit.

Character and habits

Hind bin Abi Haalah ﷽ reports that Rasulullah 襚 was always restless out of concern for the hereafter. Nabi 襚 had a soft temperament and was gentle in speech. Nabi 襚 never disgraced anyone. He never considered any gift to be insignificant. Nabi 襚 was very clear when he spoke and never spoke unnecessarily.

Nabi 襚 did not become angry with others due to personal reasons. If Nabi 襚 saw anything unpleasant, he turned his mubaarak face away. If it was something pleasant he would lower his gaze.

Hadhrat Ali ﷽ mentions that Nabi 襚 refrained from all speech that was evil, shameless and which portrayed an immoral message. He forgave those who treated him harshly. Nabi 襚 never raised his hands against anyone. However, if any command of Allah 襚 was violated, Nabi 襚 expressed his anger. Rasulullah 襚 would easily interact with the people of his household and would carry out the daily chores at home. He would sweep the floor and milk the goat. He attended to all his needs himself.

Nabi 襚 constantly remembered Allah 襚 in all conditions and would always fulfill the needs of others. If Nabi 襚 did not have anything with him to give to someone, he would excuse himself in a gentle and kind tone. He also visited the sick. Nabi 襚 did not avoid sitting with the slaves or the poor.

Rasulullah 襚 loved good fragrances and disliked bad odours. Nabi 襚 greeted everyone with a cheerful face. He never found fault with food. Often, there would be starvation in the house of Nabi 襚. His family never ate barley bread to their fill. At times there was such starvation, that for two months not even a fire was lit in the house of Nabi 襚.

Mu'jizaat (miracles)

Allah ﷻ caused certain miracles to take place at the hands of His Ambiyaa. This would be a sign of their nubuwat, causing their opposition and enemies to lower their heads in submission before them.

There were numerous mu`jizaat shown at the hands of our Nabi ﷺ.

The mu'jizaat of the past Ambiyaa were restricted to their lifetimes, whereas the mu'jizah of our Nabi ﷺ, which is the Qur'aan is present until today and will remain until Qiyaamah. All other powers are powerless in front of it.

Besides this great mu`jizah, there were other mu`jizaat such as the splitting of the moon into two, flowing of water from the mubaarak fingers of Nabi ﷺ and stones and trees making salaam to Nabi ﷺ. The crying of the date trunk, which was used by Nabi ﷺ to lean against is also a great mu'jizah of our Master ﷺ. There is also the incident of Rasulullah ﷺ calling the trees which responded to his call and then returned to their spots. There are thousands of mu'jizaat and predictions of Rasulullah ﷺ that are clearly recorded. The Ulama have written separate books on this subject.

May Allah Ta'ala imbibe in us the love of our Noble Master, Sayyidinah wa Maulana Muhammad ﷺ. *Aameen.*

30992379R00048

Printed in Great Britain
by Amazon